Disclaimer

Book Title: Codes for the Identification of Federal and Federally-Assisted Organization

Book Author: William C. Barker; Hildegard Ferraiolo

Book Abstract: The Homeland Security Presidential Directive HSPD-12 called for new standards to be adopted governing the interoperable use of identity credentials to allow physical and logical access to Federal government locations and systems. The Personal Identity Verification (PIV) for Federal Employees and Contractors, (Federal Information Processing Standard 201 (FIPS 201)) was developed to establish standards for identity credentials. This document, Special Publication 800-87 (SP 800-87), provides the organizational codes necessary to establish the PIV Federal Agency Smart Credential Number (PIV FASC-N) that is required to be included in the FIPS 201 Card Holder Unique Identifier (CHUID) and is a companion document to FIPS 201.

Citation: NIST SP - 800-87rev1

Keyword: HSPD-12; PIV; PACS; FIPS 201; identity credentials; Smart Card; personal identification verification

NIST Special Publication 800-87
Revision 1 -2008

Codes for Identification of
Federal and Federally-Assisted
Organizations

**National Institute of
Standards and Technology**
U.S. Department of Commerce

**William C. Barker
Hildegard Ferraiolo**

INFORMATION SECURITY

Computer Security Division
Information Technology Laboratory
National Institute of Standards and Technology
Gaithersburg, MD, 20899-8930

April 2008

U.S. Department of
Carlos M. Gutierrez, Secretary

National Institute of Standards and Technology
Dr. James Turner, Acting Director

Reports on Computer Systems Technology

The Information Technology Laboratory (ITL) at the National Institute of Standards and Technology (NIST) promotes the U.S. economy and public welfare by providing technical leadership for the Nation's measurement and standards infrastructure. ITL develops tests, test methods, reference data, proof of concept implementations, and technical analyses to advance the development and productive use of information technology. ITL's responsibilities include the development of management, administrative, technical, and physical standards and guidelines for the cost-effective security and privacy of non-national security-related information in Federal information systems. This special publication 800-series reports on ITL's research, guidelines, and outreach efforts in information system security, and its collaborative activities with industry, government, and academic organizations.

Certain commercial entities, equipment, or materials may be identified in this
document in order to describe an experimental procedure or concept adequately.
Such identification is not intended to imply recommendation or endorsement by the
National Institute of Standards and Technology, nor is it intended to imply that the
entities, materials, or equipment are necessarily the best available for the purpose.

National Institute of Standards and Technology Special Publication 800-87, Revision 1, April 2008 edition
Natl. Inst. Stand. Technol. Spec. Publ. 800-87 Revision 1, 103 pages (April 2008)

Executive Summary

The Homeland Security Presidential Directive HSPD-12 called for new standards to be adopted governing the interoperable use of identity credentials to allow physical and logical access to Federal government locations and systems. *The Personal Identity Verification (PIV) for Federal Employees and Contractors*, (Federal Information Processing Standard 201 (FIPS 201)) was developed to establish standards for identity credentials. This document, Special Publication 800-87 (SP 800-87), provides the organizational codes necessary to establish the PIV Federal Agency Smart Credential Number (PIV FASC-N) that is required to be included in the FIPS 201 Card Holder Unique Identifier (CHUID) and is a companion document to FIPS 201.

Table of Contents

1   Introduction

1.1   Authority

The National Institute of Standards and Technology (NIST) developed this document in furtherance of its statutory responsibilities under the Federal Information Security Management Act (FISMA) of 2002, Public Law 107-347.

NIST is responsible for developing standards and guidelines, including minimum requirements, for providing adequate information security for all agency operations and assets; but such standards and guidelines shall not apply to national security systems. This recommendation is consistent with the requirements of the Office of Management and Budget (OMB) Circular A-130, Section 8b(3), Securing Agency Information Systems" as analyzed in A-130, Appendix IV: Analysis of Key Sections. Supplemental information is provided in A-130, Appendix III.

This recommendation has been prepared for use by federal agencies. It may be used by nongovernmental organizations on a voluntary basis and is not subject to copyright. Nothing in this document should be taken to contradict standards and guidelines made mandatory and binding on federal agencies by the Secretary of Commerce under statutory authority. Nor should this recommendation be interpreted as altering or superseding the existing authorities of the Secretary of Commerce, Director of the OMB, or any other federal official.

1.2   Purpose and Scope

FIPS 201 was developed to establish standards for identity credentials for Federal employees and Federal contractors. This document provides the organizational codes for federal agencies to establish the Federal Agency Smart Credential Number (FASC-N) that is required to be included in the FIPS 201 Card Holder Unique Identifier. SP 800-87 is a companion document to FIPS 201. All changes implemented in this publication are listed in Appendix A.

1.3   Maintenance Organization

The maintenance organization for codes for the identification of federal and federally assisted organizations for the PIV FASC-N is the Department of Commerce in coordination with the General Services Administration and the Departments of Homeland Security and Commerce. Federal departments and independent agencies are invited to assist in the maintenance of this publication by submitting copies of newly implemented tables of organization that affect any listing. Such changes should be submitted to the National Institute of Standards and Technology (NIST) through the online request form located at http://piv.nist.gov/ or via e-mail to PIV_comments@nist.gov with "SP 800-87 Update Request " in the subject line.

The two leftmost characters of each code form a component data element which is identical with the two-digit numerical code used in the federal budgetary process to identify major federal organizations. This component, designated as the Treasury Agency Symbol (TAS), is maintained by the U.S. Department of the Treasury; and the National Archives and Records Administration legislatively owns the records.

1.4   Applicability

This document is targeted at Federal agencies and implementers of PIV systems for the establishment of the PIV FASC-N organizational codes. This publication is not intended for the replacement of U.S. Department of the Treasury agency location and appropriation fund account codes.

1.5   Organizational Structure

This publication provides a four-character PIV FASC-N organizational code for each organization listed. The major set of categories used to distinguish groups of organizations in this publication is the following:

Legislative Branch,

Judicial Branch,

Executive Office and Departments (and their Associated Organizations)

Other Independent federal and Quasi-federal Organizations (and their Associated Organizations)

Independent federal-State and Interstate Organizations

International Organizations.

Organizational structure is described and encoded in this publication in a manner consistent with the budgetary structure of the U.S. Government. Consistency with the budgetary structure has been maintained in order to permit the adoption of the two-digit numerical code used in the budgetary process to identify most first-level, independent federal organizations. This coding system is maintained by the U.S. Department of the Treasury. Designated as the Treasury Agency Symbol (TAS), it serves as the two leftmost characters of the organization code used in this publication.

All first-level organizations in each of the above categories are listed in this publication. A first-level organization is not subsumed hierarchically under any other organization. Second-level organizations are included with the Executive Office, executive departments, and certain other major agencies. Third- and lower-level organizations are included only in the Department of Defense and in special situations in other departments. Second-, third-, and lower-level organizations are always subsumed hierarchically under a next-higher-level organization.

In this publication, an "independent" organization is defined as having both hierarchical independence and budgetary independence, i.e., it is first-level (hierarchical independence) and has a budget which is not subsumed by or connected in a subsidiary manner with the budget of another organization (budgetary independence). An "associated" organization is first-level, but has no budgetary independence. The five types of associated organizations are:

Associated federal Organizations, which are federal agencies or their ancillary units such as advisory committees; they are often included as part of the independent organizations to which they are related

Associated federal-State Organizations, which are associated organizations in which the federal Government and one or more States participate jointly

2

Government-Sponsored Enterprises, which are so identified in a separate section of the Budget of the United States Government, Appendix (referred to as The Budget)

Federally Aided Organizations, which are domestic and non-federal, and are identified in The Budget as receiving some form of financial support such as a direct payment, loan guarantee, line of credit, or stock purchase arrangement

International Organizations, identified in The Budget or in the Department of State's annual report of United States Contributions to International Organizations as organizations in which the federal Government serves as a financial contributor.

A "quasi-federal" organization is an organization that is listed as "quasi-official" in the U.S. Government Manual and is also assigned its own unique TAS code by the U.S. Department of the Treasury. An "interstate" organization included in this publication is federally assisted but differs from a federal-State organization in that it involves no federal participation.

Associated organizations and organizations below the first level usually carry the same TAS as the independent, first-level organization with which they are connected. Organizations having the same TAS are distinguished from each other by the two rightmost characters of the identifier. These characters are alphanumeric, although numeric characters are being used at this time in most cases. The recommended system used for assignment of the two rightmost characters of the identifier is explained below in Section 4: Special Information.

2   Specifications: Table of Organizations and Codes

2.1   Part A: Arrangement by Hierarchical and Budgetary Relationship

In this part, names of first-level organizations are presented immediately to the right of the assigned codes without an indentation.

Second-level organizations are listed immediately below the first-level organization to which they report and are indented further to the right. Second-level organizations which subdivide a first-level organization form a complete, non-duplicative set, i.e., each employee of the first-level organization can be assigned to one and only one second-level entry.

Third- and lower-level organizations are indented further to the right than their respective next-higher level entries, and they are listed immediately below the entry that they subdivide. Third- and lower-level entries, similarly, form a complete, non-duplicative set.

At any level for which entries are provided, some subdivisions may not be individually identified. Those divisions not specifically listed are included by implication, as in "Office of the Assistant Secretary for Health except National Centers."

Each domestic, associated organization is listed with the independent organization with which its financial or administrative support is connected. International organizations are listed in a separate section.

2.2   Part B: Arrangement by Alphanumeric Sequence of Assigned Codes

Part B is a listing of organizations and codes arranged by alphanumeric sequence of codes.

3   Qualifications

This document, Special Publication 800-87 (SP 800-87), provides the organizational codes for Federal Agencies to establish the Federal Agency Smart Credential Number (FASC-N) that is required to be included in the FIPS 201 Card Holder Unique Identifier (CHUID). Because FIPS 201 applies only to federal agencies, non-federal organizations were excluded from the requirements of this Special Publication. Users desiring a compatible code assignment to an initially excluded organization may assign their own four-character code, preferably with a letter as the leftmost character to avoid possible conflict with the numerical TAS.

4   Special Information

The coding structure in this publication is based on the establishment of four active classes of TAS codes. The assignments of the two rightmost characters of the identifier differ in each of the classes and are described below.

Defense TAS Codes

The following TAS codes are used to identify component organizations of the Department of Defense:

- 17: Department of the Navy;
- 21: Department of the Army;
- 57: Department of the Air Force;
- 84: U.S. Soldiers' and Airmen's Home;
- 96: U.S. Corps of Engineers--(civil); and
- 97: Department of Defense as a whole and components, other than the military department, reporting to the Secretary of Defense.

Values of the two rightmost characters of the identifier for all component organizations of the Department of Defense (DoD) are received from the Directorate for Information Resources Management Systems, Office of the Assistant Secretary of Defense (Comptroller). DoD assigns their own codes, usually alphabetic (can be numeric).

Joint-Use TAS Codes

Several non-Defense, independent organizations share certain TAS codes. These organizations are fully distinguished at the first level by the third and fourth characters of the identifier. The TAS codes in this class, and their applications, are:

- 00: Senate and House of Representatives;
- 09: Smaller Legislative Agencies;
- 10: Judicial Agencies;
- 46: Independent federal-State and Interstate Organizations (excepting Advisory Commission on Intergovernmental Relations);
- 48: Temporary Study Commissions;
- 76: Historical and Memorial Agencies; and
- 95: Other Independent Organizations Not Assigned Unique TAS Codes.

TAS Code 11: Executive Office of the President/Funds Appropriated to the President

The Executive Office of the President is assigned identifier 1100, and agencies within the Office are assigned identifiers in the range of 1101 through 1130. The office of the Vice President is assigned 1160.

Agencies that come under the "Funds Appropriated to the President" (FAP) in the federal Budget also are assigned TAS code 11. Currently, two different ranges are used for the two rightmost characters for these FAP agencies. Agencies that are international in scope, such as the Multilateral Development Banks, are assigned alphabetic characters consistent with other international agencies. Other FAP agencies, such as the Peace Corps, are assigned numerics for the two rightmost characters. These currently range from 31 to 62.

For values of the two rightmost characters of the identifier for associated organizations using TAS code 11, see below under "Single-Use TAS Codes." This class of TAS codes includes all codes that are active (i.e., in current use) and not identified above in another class. As implied in the class name, an independent organization using a TAS code in this class does not share that TAS code with any other independent organization. Second-level, third-level, and associated organizations may be included in this class and will use the same TAS codes as their respective independent organizations.

For each TAS code in this class, the two rightmost characters of the identifier are recommended to be assigned as follows:

> 00: organization as a whole (always present);
> 01: office of the chief executive and any staff functions not separately identified;
> 02: office of the deputy chief executive;
> 03: office of the general counsel or equivalent;
> 04: office of the inspector general;
> 05: office of administration or management, if no "planning" or "policy" functions are included in the name;
> 06: office of policy, evaluation, or program analysis, including any "budget" functions not included in "administration" or "management";
> 07: office of Congressional and legislative affairs; may include public or intergovernmental affairs if not separately identified;
> 08: office of public affairs, if identified separately from Congressional and legislative affairs;
> 09: office of international affairs;
> 10 through 29: other staff offices;
> 30 through 59: programmatic or line organizations, and all of their separately identified, lower-level components;
> 60 through 69: Associated federal Organizations;
> 70 through 79: Associated federal-State Organizations;
> 80 through 89: Government-Sponsored Enterprises;
> 90 through 99: Federally Aided Organizations; and
> AA through ZZ: International Organizations.

For the assignment of the two rightmost characters to international organizations, groupings of such organizations have been established. The third character of the identifier is the same for each organization in a group. This permits recognition of an identifier as pertaining to a particular group. For example, inter-American organizations have the two rightmost characters of their identifiers in the range AA through AZ; international fisheries organizations are assigned the range FA through FZ, while United Nations and affiliated agencies are assigned the range UA through UZ. This procedure for assigning the two rightmost characters of the identifier is used for each international organization, regardless of the TAS code assigned to the organization.

If expansion of the coding structure is required due to saturation, the fourth or rightmost character of the identifier will be converted to an alphanumeric for staff, line, and domes associated organizations under Single-Use TAS Codes. Then, more identifiers for these types of organizations would be available. For example, in this expansion, the two rightmost characters of identifiers for line organizations under Single-Use TAS Codes could include code 2A through 5Z as well as 20 through 59, while the two rightmost characters for associated federal organizations could include codes 6A through 6Z as well as 60 through 69. This expansion could apply, in a similar fashion, to the coding structure for domestic organization under TAS code 11 or the Joint-Use TAS Codes.

Table of Organizations and Codes

Part A: Arrangement by Hierarchical and Budgetary Relationship

TABLE OF ORGANIZATIONS AND CODES
LEGISLATIVE BRANCH

Code Organization

0000 THE LEGISLATIVE BRANCH

<u>Congress</u>

0001   Congress, generally, no additional specification available

0010 Senate,   The

0050   House of Representatives, The

0099   Joint House and Senate Entities
      (Capitol Police Board, Capitol Guide Service, Office of the Attending
      Physician, Joint Economic Committee, Joint Committee on Printing,
      and Joint Committee on Taxation)

<u>Major Legislative Agencies</u>

0100   Architect of the Capitol

0800   Congressional Budget Office

0500   General Accounting Office
0501   Comptroller General of the United States
0559   GAO, except Comptroller General

0400   Government Printing Office

0300   Library of Congress

<u>Associated Federal Organizations:</u>

0361   Library of Congress Trust Fund Board
0363   Federal Library & Information Center Committee

2300   U.S. Tax Court

9593   U.S. Court of Appeals for Veterans Claims

TABLE OF ORGANIZATIONS AND CODES
LEGISLATIVE BRANCH
Code Organization

LEGISLATIVE BRANCH - Continued

Smaller Legislative Agencies

0902 Botanic   Garden

0901   Commission on Security and Cooperation in Europe

0914   John C. Stennis Center for Public Service Training and Development

0904   Office of Compliance

0962   Permanent Committee for the Oliver Wendell Holmes Devise

0929   U.S. Capitol Preservation Commission

TABLE OF ORGANIZATIONS AND CODES
LEGISLATIVE BRANCH

Code Organization

1000   **THE JUDICIAL BRANCH**

1001   Supreme Court of the United States
1050   Chief Justice of the United States
1051 Associate   Justices of the Supreme Court
1059   Supreme Court, except Justices

~~Associated Federal Organization:~~

1060   Judicial Conference of the United States

1002   U.S. Courts of Appeals-Judicial Circuits
          (except Federal Circuit)

1003   U.S. Court of Appeals for the Federal Circuit

1004   U.S. Court of International Trade

1005   U.S. Court of Federal Claims

1012   U.S. District and Territorial Courts

1018   U.S. Judicial Panel on Multidistrict Litigation

1021 Bankruptcy   Courts

1023   Federal Public Defenders

1025 Court   Security

1027   Administrative Office of the U.S. Courts

1028   Federal Judicial Center

1030   United States Sentencing Commission

TABLE OF ORGANIZATIONS AND CODES
EXECUTIVE DEPARTMENTS
(and their associated organizations)

Code Organization

1100　**EXECUTIVE OFFICE OF THE PRESIDENT**

1101　President of the United States

1102　National Security Council

1103　Office of Management and Budget
1121　Director,　　OMB
1129　　　OMB, except Director

1105　Office of Administration

1109　Office of the United States Trade Representative

1110　Office of Policy Development

1112　Office of Science and Technology Policy

1113　Council of Economic Advisors

1117　White House Office

1118　Executive Residence at the White House

1119　Council on Environmental Quality/Office of Environmental Quality

1127　Office of the National Drug Control Policy

1160　Office of the Vice President of the United States

1140　President's Council on Sustainable Development

1148　Office of Homeland Security

1170　Commission on the Intelligence Capabilities of the United States Regarding
　　　Weapons of Mass Destruction

Associated Federal Organizations:

TABLE OF ORGANIZATIONS AND CODES
EXECUTIVE DEPARTMENTS
(and their associated organizations)

Code Organization

1165   White House Commission on Presidential Scholars

TABLE OF ORGANIZATIONS AND CODES
EXECUTIVE DEPARTMENTS
(and their associated organizations)

Code Organization

1200	**AGRICULTURE**, Department of
1201	Office of the Secretary of Agriculture
12J0	Assistant Secretary for Congressional Relations
12J2	USDA, Office of Congressional and Intergovernmental Relations
1205	USDA, Office of the Chief Financial Officer
1208	USDA, Office of Communications
12A0	USDA, Office of Executive Operations
12A2	USDA, Office of Executive Secretariat
12A4	USDA, Homeland Security
12A5	USDA, Office of the Chief Economist
12A6	USDA, Office of Budget and Program Analysis
12A9	USDA, National Appeals Division
12A7	USDA, Office of the Chief Information Officer
1203	USDA, Office of the General Counsel
1204	Office of the Inspector General
12A8	USDA, Office of Small and Disadvantaged Business
12B1	USDA, Office of Security Services
12B2	USDA, Civil Rights
12B3	USDA, Office of Property and Procurement Management
12B5	USDA, Office of Human Capital Management
12B6	USDA, Office of the Administrative Law Judge
12B7	USDA, Office of the Judicial Officer
12B8	USDA, Board of Contract Appeals
12BD	USDA, Office of Ethics
1215	USDA, Office of Operations
12B0	USDA, Assistant Secretary for Administration
12C0	Under Secretary for Natural Resources and Environment
12C2	Forest Service
12C3	Natural Resources Conservation Service
12D0	Under Secretary for Farm and Foreign Agricultural Services
12D2	Farm Service Agency
12D3	Foreign Agricultural Service
12D4	Risk Management Agency
1263	Federal Crop Insurance Corporation
1260	Commodity Credit Corporation
12E0	Under Secretary for Rural Development

TABLE OF ORGANIZATIONS AND CODES
EXECUTIVE DEPARTMENTS
(and their associated organizations)

Code Organization

1200	**AGRICULTURE**, Department of - continued
12E2	Rural Utilities Service
1261	Rural Telephone Bank
12E3	Rural Housing Service
12E4	Rural Business Cooperative Service
12E6	National Sheep Industry Improvement Center
12F0	Under Secretary for Food, Nutrition, and Consumer Services
12F2	Food and Nutrition Service
12F3	Center for Nutrition Policy and Promotion
12G0	Under Secretary for Food Safety
12G2	Food Safety and Inspection Service
12H0	Under Secretary for Research, Education, and Economics
12H2	Agricultural Research Service
12H3	Cooperative State Research, Education, and Extension Service
12H4	Economic Research Service
12H5	National Agricultural Statistics Service
12K0	Under Secretary for Marketing and Regulatory Programs
12K2	Agricultural Marketing Service
12K3	Animal and Plant Health Inspection Service
12K4	Grain Inspection, Packers and Stockyards Administration

Federally Aided Organization:

1291	Land grant colleges and Tuskegee Institute

TABLE OF ORGANIZATIONS AND CODES
EXECUTIVE DEPARTMENTS
(and their associated organizations)

Code Organization

1300   **COMMERCE**, Department of

     1301   Office of the Secretary
     1303   Office of the General Counsel
     1304   Office of the Inspector General
     1306   Office of the Chief Financial Officer & Assistant Secretary for Administration
     1314   Economic and Statistics Administration/Under Secretary for Economic Affairs
     1321   Bureau of Economic Analysis
     1323   Bureau of the Census
     1315   Chief   Economist
     1325   Economic Development Administration/Assistant Secretary for Economic Development
     1350   International Trade Administration/Under Secretary for International Trade
     1351   Under Secretary for Export Administration/Bureau of Industry and Security
     1359   Technology   Administration/Under Secretary of Technology
     1341   National Institute of Standards and Technology
     1342   National Technical Information Service
     1343   Assistant Secretary for Technology Policy
     1330   National Oceanic and Atmospheric Administration/Under Secretary for Oceans and Atmosphere
     1335   National Telecommunication and Information Administration/Assistant Secretary for Communications and Information
     1344   Patent and Trademark Office/Under Secretary for Intellectual Property
     1352   Minority Business Development Agency

       Associated Federal Organizations:

     1363   Committee for the Implementation of Textile Agreements
     1365   Export Administration Review Board

TABLE OF ORGANIZATIONS AND CODES
EXECUTIVE DEPARTMENTS
(and their associated organizations)

Code Organization

9700 **DEFENSE**, Department of (except military departments)

Office of the Secretary of Defense and related Organizations

97AD	Office of the Secretary of Defense
97EX	Office of the Inspector General
97BJ	Organization of the Joint Chiefs of Staff

DEFENSE   AGENCIES

97AE	Defense Advanced Research Projects Agency
97JC	Missile Defense Agency
9759	Consolidated Metropolitan Technical Personnel Center
97AZ	Defense Commissary Agency
97AR	Defense Contract Audit Agency
9763	Defense Contract Management Agency
97BZ	Defense Finance and Accounting Service
97AK	Defense Information Systems Agency
97DL	Defense Intelligence Agency
97AV	Defense Security Service
97AQ	Defense Legal Services Agency
97AS	Defense Logistics Agency
97AB	National Geospatial-Intelligence Agency
97AT	Defense Security Cooperation Agency
97CG	National Security Agency/Central Security Service
9761	Defense Threat Reduction Agency
9762	Defense Career Management and Support Agency
9765	Pentagon Force Protection Agency

Field Activities of the Department of Defense

97F1	American Forces Information Service
9758	Defense Prisoner of War/Missing Personnel Office
97AU	Defense Technology Security Administration
9748	Defense Human Resources Activity
97F2	Department of Defense Education Activity
97F6	Office of Economic Adjustment
97F5	Washington Headquarters Services
9760	TRICARE Management Activity

TABLE OF ORGANIZATIONS AND CODES
EXECUTIVE DEPARTMENTS
(and their associated organizations)

Code Organization

9700   **DEFENSE**, Department of (except military departments) - continued

9766   Department of Defense Counterintelligence Field Activity
9774   Defense Technical Information Center

Other Activities/Organizations

97GZ   U.S. Court of Appeals for the Armed Forces
9736   Army/Air Force Exchange Service
9767   Unified Combatant Command Headquarters
9769   National Defense University
9770   Armed Forces Radiobiology Research Institute
9771   Defense Microelectronics Activity
9772   Pentagon Renovation Program Office
9773   Virginia Contracting Activity

TABLE OF ORGANIZATIONS AND CODES
EXECUTIVE DEPARTMENTS
(and their associated organizations)

Code Organization

5700 **AIR FORCE**, Department of the (Headquarters, USAF)

5701	Air Force Management Engineering Agency
5702	Air Force Inspection and Safety Center
5703	Air Force Operational Test and Evaluation Center
5704	Air Force Communications Agency
5705	Air Force Intelligence Service
5706	Air Force Audit Agency
5707	Air Force Office of Special Investigations
5708	Air Force Office of Security Police
5709	Air Force Personnel Center
5711	Air Force Manpower Agency
570B	U.S. Air Force Academy
570D	U.S. Air Forces, Europe
570J	Air Training Command
570K	Air University
570M	Headquarters, Air Force Reserve
570N	Immediate Office, Headquarters, USAF
570R	Pacific Air Forces
570U	Air Force Headquarters Air Intelligence Agency
570Y	Air Force Communications Command
571A	Air Force C2 & Intelligence, Surveillance & Reconnaissance
571C	Air Combat Command
571G	Air Force Logistics Management Agency
571L	Air Mobility Command
571M	Air Force Materiel Command
571O	Air Force Center for Quality and Management Innovation
571P	Air Force Real Property Agency
571Q	HQ AF Flight Standards Agency
571S	Space Command
571W	Air Force Engineering and Services Center
5727	Air Force Agency for Modeling and Simulation
5728	Air Force Communication and Information Center
5729	Air Force National Security Emergency Preparedness
572A	Air Force Cost Center
572B	Air Force Doctrine Center
572C	Air Force Civilian Personnel Management Center
572D	Air Force Personnel Operations Agency
572E	Air Force Legal Services Center

TABLE OF ORGANIZATIONS AND CODES
EXECUTIVE DEPARTMENTS
(and their associated organizations)

Code Organization

5700   **AIR FORCE**, Department of the (Headquarters, USAF) - continued

572F	Air Force Medical Services Center
572G	Air Force Service Information and News Center
572H	Air Force Combat Operations Staff
572K	U.S. Air Force Historical Research Center
572L	Air Force Technical Applications Center
572M	Air Force Review Boards Office
572N	Air Force Center for Studies and Analyses
572P	Air Force Center for International Programs
572Q	Air Weather Service
572R	Air Force Program Executive Office
572S	HQ NORAD
572T	Air Force Supply Center
572U	Air Force Morale, Welfare and Recreation Center
572V	Air Force Disposal Agency
572W	Air Force District of Washington
572X	Air Force Real Estate Agency
572Y	Air Force Pentagon Communications Agency
572Z	HQ Air Force Medical Operations Agency
573C	Air Force Elements, U.S. Central Command
573D	Air Force Elements, U.S. Special Operations Command
573G	Air Force Elements, Europe
573I	Reservist, Centrally Managed
573K	HQ U.S. European Command
573L	Center for Air Force History
573M	Air Force Elements, U.S. Southern Command
573N	Air Force Elements, U.S. Atlantic Command
573O	Air Force Elements, U.S. Pacific Command
573Q	Air Force Elements, U.S. Strategic Command
573R	Air Force Elements, U.S. Readiness Command
573S	Headquarters, U.S. Space Command and NORAD
573T	Air Force Elements U.S. Transportation Command
573V	Air Force Elements, Other than Europe
573W	Air Force Center for Environmental Excellence
573Y	Air Force Frequency Management Center
573Z	Joint Services Survival, Evasion, Resistance and Escape Agency

TABLE OF ORGANIZATIONS AND CODES
EXECUTIVE DEPARTMENTS
(and their associated organizations)

Code Organization

5700   **AIR FORCE**, Department of the (Headquarters, USAF) - continued

Code	Organization
574Z	Air National Guard
572I	Air National Guard Support Center
5734	Air National Guard Units (Mobilization) (Title 5)
57NG	Air National Guard Units (Title 32)
57ZG U.S.	Special Operations Command (ANG Title 32)
57ZS	U.S. Special Operations Command (Air Force)
570I	Air Reserve Personnel Center

TABLE OF ORGANIZATIONS AND CODES
EXECUTIVE DEPARTMENTS
(and their associated organizations)

Code Organization

2100   **ARMY**, Department of the (except Corps of Engineers Civil Program Financing)

21SA   Office of the Secretary of the Army
21SB   Field Operating Offices of the Office of the Secretary of the Army
21SE   Field Operating Agencies of the Army Staff Resourced through OA-22
21SF   Field Operating Agencies of the Army Staff
21SJ   Joint Services and Activities Supported by the Office, Secretary of the Army
21G6   U.S. Army Network Enterprise Technology Command/9th Army Signal
       Command

Office of the Chief of Staff of the Army

21CS   Immediate Office of the Chief of Staff of the Army
21BA   U.S. Army Installation Management Agency
21AE   Acquisition Executive Support Command Agency
21P8   Eighth U.S. Army
21JA   Joint Activities
21PC   Military Entrance Processing Command
21MT   Military Traffic Management Command

2130   National Guard Bureau
21GB   Office of the Chief of the National Guard Bureau
21NG   Army National Guard Units (Title 32)
21MD   Surgeon General
21AU   U.S. Army Audit Agency
21CE   U.S. Army Corps of Engineers, except civil program financing
96CE   U.S. Army Corps of Engineers - civil program financing only
21CB   U.S. Army Criminal Investigation Command
21J1   U.S. Army Element SHAPE

U.S. Army Europe and Seventh Army
21E1   Immediate Office of the Commander-In-Chief of the U.S. Army
        Europe and Seventh Army
21E2   21st Theater Army Area Command
21E3   U.S. Army Southern European Task Force
21E5   U.S.   Army V Corps
21EB   1st   Personnel Command
21ED   U.S. Military Community Activity, Heidelberg
21EN   Seventh Army Training Command

TABLE OF ORGANIZATIONS AND CODES
EXECUTIVE DEPARTMENTS
(and their associated organizations)

Code Organization

2100   **ARMY**, Department of the
          (except Corps of Engineers Civil program financing) - continued

        Office of the Chief of Staff of the Army - Continued

Code	Organization
21EO	59th Ordnance Brigade
21FC	U.S. Army Forces Command
21HS	U.S. Army Health Services Command
21CZ	U.S. Army Information Systems Command
21AS	U.S. Army Intelligence and Security Command
21X1	U.S. Army Materiel Command (AMC)
21X2	Headquarters, Army Materiel Command
21X3	Headquarters, Staff Support Activities, AMC
21XK	Materiel Acquisition Activities
21XL	Materiel Acquisition Project Managers
21XX	Materiel Readiness Activities
21XR	U.S. Army Research, Development and Engineering Command
21X4	Training Activities, AMC
21XA	U.S. Army Chemical and Biological Defense Command
21XB	U.S. Army Chemical Materials Command
21X8	U.S. Army Communications Electronics Command
21XQ	U.S. Army Operations Support Command
21X5	U.S. Army Materiel Command, all others
21X6	U.S. Army Missile Command
21XD	U.S. Army Research Laboratory Command
21XP	U.S. Army Security Assistance Command
21X9	U.S. Army Simulation, Training and Instrumentation Command
21XC	U.S. Army Soldiers System Command (SSC)
21X7	U.S. Army Tank-Automotive and Armament Command (TACOM)
21XT	U.S. Army Test, Measurement, and Diagnostic Equipment Activity
21MC	U.S. Army Medical Command
21MW	U.S. Army Military District of Washington
21RC	U.S. Army Recruiting Command

TABLE OF ORGANIZATIONS AND CODES
EXECUTIVE DEPARTMENTS
(and their associated organizations)

Code Organization

2100   **ARMY**, Department of the
(except Corps of Engineers Civil program financing) - continued

Office of the Chief of Staff of the Army - continued

Code	Organization
21HR	U.S. Army Reserve Command
21SU	U.S. Army Southern Command
21FL	U.S. Army South Command
21SC	U.S. Army Space and Strategic Defense Command
21AT	U.S. Army Test and Evaluation Command
21TC	U.S. Army Training and Doctrine Command
21P1	U.S. Army, Pacific
21MA	U.S. Military Academy
21SP	U.S. Special Operation Command (Army)
21MP	U.S. Army Human Resources Command
21SS	Staff Support Agencies of the Chief of Staff, Army

Associated Federal Organization:

9668 Mississippi   River Commission

TABLE OF ORGANIZATIONS AND CODES
EXECUTIVE DEPARTMENTS
(and their associated organizations)

Code Organization

1700 **NAVY**, Department of the

1712   Navy Secretariat/Staff Offices
1708   Immediate Office of the Secretary of the Navy
1710 Navy   Field Offices
1709 Navy   Staff Offices
1714   Office of Naval Research

          Chief of Naval Operations

1711   Immediate Office of the Chief of Naval Operations
1715   Naval Intelligence Command
1718   Naval Medical Command
1719   Naval Air Systems Command
1722   Bureau of Naval Personnel
1723   Naval Supply Systems Command
1724   Naval Sea Systems Command
1725   Naval Facilities Engineering Command
1730   Special Projects Office
1733   Military Sealift Command
1739   Naval Space and Warfare Systems Command
1741   Naval Systems Management Activity
1752   Commander, Navy Installations
1760   U.S. Atlantic Fleet, Commander In Chief
1761   U.S. Naval Forces, Europe
1762   Chief of Naval Education and Training
1763   Naval Network Operations Command
1765   Naval Oceanography Command
1769   Naval Security Group Command
1770   U.S. Pacific Fleet, Commander in Chief
1772   Naval Reserve Force
1774   Naval Special Warfare Command
17ZS   U.S. Special Operations Command (Navy)
1776   Naval Education and Training Command
1727 U.S. Marine Corps

TABLE OF ORGANIZATIONS AND CODES
EXECUTIVE DEPARTMENTS
(and their associated organizations)

Code Organization

9100   **EDUCATION**, Department of

9101   Immediate Office of the Secretary of Education
9102   Office of the Deputy Secretary of Education
9108   Office of the Under Secretary
9103   Office of the General Counsel
9104   Office of Inspector General
9105   Office of Management
9115   Office of the Chief Information Officer
9106   Office of the Chief Financial Officer
9107   Office of Legislation and Congressional Affairs
9109   Office of Communications and Outreach
9110   Office of Planning, Evaluation and Program Development
9111   Office for Civil Rights
9121   Office of English Language Acquisition
9139   Institute of Education Sciences
9132   Immediate Office of the Director of Education Sciences
9138   National Center for Education Statistics
9135   National Center for Education Research
9137   National Center for Educational Evaluation and Regional Assistance
9136   National Center for Special Education Research
9131   Federal Student Aid
9146   Office of Elementary and Secondary Education
9141   Immediate Office of the Assistant Secretary
                 for Elementary and Secondary Education
9140   Student Achievement and School Accountability Program
9145   Office of Indian Education
9142   Migrant Education Programs
9144   Impact Aid Programs
9143   School Support and Technology Programs
9147   Academic Improvement and Teacher Quality Programs
9134   Office of Postsecondary Education
9130   Immediate Office of the Assistant Secretary for Postsecondary Education
9129   Fund for the Improvement of Postsecondary Education
9133   Office of Higher Education Programs
9124   Office of Special Education and Rehabilitative Services
9128   Immediate Office of the Assistant Secretary
                 for Special Education and Rehabilitative Services
9125   National Institute on Disability and Rehabilitation Research
9126   Rehabilitation Services Administration

TABLE OF ORGANIZATIONS AND CODES
EXECUTIVE DEPARTMENTS
(and their associated organizations)

Code Organization

9100   **EDUCATION**, Department of – continued

9127   Office of Special Education Programs
9120   Office of Vocational and Adult Education
9150   Office of Innovation and Improvement
9155   Office of Safe and Drug-Free Schools

Associated Federal Organizations:

916A   Advisory Councils and Committees
916B   National Assessment Governing Board
916C   National Institute for Literacy
916D   Federal Interagency Committee on Education

Government-Sponsored Enterprise:

9181   Student Loan Marketing Association (Sallie Mae)
9182   College Construction Loan Insurance Association (Connie Lee)

Federally Aided Organizations:

9191   American Printing House for the Blind
9192 Gallaudet   University
9193 Howard   University
9194   National Technical Institute for the Deaf

TABLE OF ORGANIZATIONS AND CODES
EXECUTIVE DEPARTMENTS
(and their associated organizations)

Code Organization

8900	**ENERGY**, Department of
8901	Office of the Secretary
8903	Office of General Counsel
8904	Office of Inspector General
893C	Office of the Chief Financial Officer
891N	Office of Chief Information Officer
8905	Assistant Secretary for Congressional and Intergovernmental Affairs
8915	Office of Public Affairs
8938	Assistant Secretary for Policy and International Affairs
891C	Office of Economic Impact and Diversity
8906	Office of Hearings and Appeals
893H	Office of Human Capital Management
8929	Office of Intelligence
892E	Office of the Secretary of Energy Advisory Board
891H	Office of Health, Safety and Security
893M	Office of Management
892H	Office of Counterintelligence
892L	Office of Electricity Delivery and Energy Reliability
8932	Office of Energy Information Administration
8936	Office of Legacy Management
891S	Office of the Departmental Representative to the Defense Nuclear Facilities Safety Board
8921	Assistant Secretary for Energy Efficiency and Renewable Energy
8911	Office of Civilian Radioactive Waste Management
8917	Assistant Secretary for Environmental Management
8928	Assistant Secretary for Fossil Energy
8927	Office of Nuclear Energy, Science and Technology

National Nuclear Security Administration (NNSA)

89NA	Office of the National Nuclear Security Administrator
89N0	Deputy Under Secretary for Counterterrorism
89N2	Deputy Administrator for Defense Nuclear Nonproliferation
89N1	Deputy Administration for Defense Programs
89N3	Deputy Administrator for Naval Reactors
89N4	Office of Emergency Operations
89N5	Associate Administrator for Facilities and Operations

TABLE OF ORGANIZATIONS AND CODES
EXECUTIVE DEPARTMENTS
(and their associated organizations)

Code Organization

8900   **ENERGY**, Department of - continued

89N6   Associate Administrator for Management and Administration
89N7   Associate Administrator for Defense Nuclear Security
89NW   Oakland Operations Office (NNSA) (EM)
89X1   Pittsburgh Naval Reactors
89X2   Schenectady Naval Reactors
89XQ   Y-12 Site Office
89XR   Pantex Site Office
89XS   Sandia Site Office
89XT   Kansas City Site Office
89XU   Los Alamos Site Office
89XV   Nevada Site Office
89XW Livermore Site Office
89SV   Savannah River Site Office
89ZA   National Nuclear Security Administration Service Center

Power Marketing Administrations:

89BP   Bonneville Power Marketing Administration
89SE   Southeastern Power Marketing Administration
89SW   Southwestern Power Marketing Administration
89WA   Western Area Power Marketing Administration

8925   Office of Science
            Site Offices

89BC   Ames Site Office
89BD   Argonne Site Office
89BE   Berkeley Site Office
89BF   Brookhaven Site Office
89BA   Chicago Office
89BG   Fermi Site Office
89BB   Oak Ridge Office
89BH   Pacific Northwest Site Office
89BI   Princeton Site Office
89BJ   Stanford Site Office
89BK   Thomas Jefferson Site Office

TABLE OF ORGANIZATIONS AND CODES
EXECUTIVE DEPARTMENTS
(and their associated organizations)

Code Organization

8900   **ENERGY**, Department of – continued

Field Offices:

89AL	Albuquerque Operations Office (non-NNSA) (EM)
89CB	Carlsbad Field Office
8981	Casper Naval Pet & Oil Shale Reserves
8955 Consolidated	Business Center
8982	Elk Hills Naval Pet & Oil Shale Reserves
89GO	Golden Field Office
89ID	Idaho Operations Office
89NV	Nevada Operations Office (non-National Nuclear Security Administration) (Environmental Management)
89NE	National Energy Technology Laboratory
89RP	Office of River Protection
89OH	Ohio Field Office
89PP	Portsmouth & Paducah Project Office
89RL	Richland Operations Office
89RF	Rocky Flats Project Office
89SR	Savannah River Operations Office
8974	Strategic Petroleum Reserves

Associated Federal Organizations:

8990   Federal Energy Regulatory Commission

TABLE OF ORGANIZATIONS AND CODES
EXECUTIVE DEPARTMENTS
(and their associated organizations)

Code Organization

7500 **HEALTH AND HUMAN SERVICES**, Department of

750S Office of the Secretary of Health and Human Services
7501   Immediate Office of the Secretary of Health and Human Services
7502   Office of the Deputy Secretary of Health and Human Services
7503   Office of the General Counsel
7504   Office of the Inspector General
7505   Office of Assistant Secretary for Administration and Management
7506   Office of Assistant Secretary for Planning and Evaluation
7507   Office of Assistant Secretary for Legislation
7508   Office of Assistant Secretary for Public Affairs
7511   Office for Civil Rights
7512   Office of Assistant Secretary for Public Response
7521   Office of the Surgeon General
7515   Office of Public Health and Science
7509   Office of Intergovernmental Affairs and Regional Directors
7510   Office of the Assistant Secretary for Resources and Technology
7516 Departmental   Appeals Board
7520   Public Health Service
7522   Substance Abuse and Mental Health Services Administration
7523   Centers for Disease Control and Prevention
7524   Food and Drug Administration
7525   Agency for Toxic Substances and Disease Registry
7526   Health Resources and Services Administration
7527   Indian Health Service
7528   Agency for Healthcare Research and Quality
7529   National Institutes of Health
7530 Centers   for Medicare & Medicaid Services
7545 Administration on Aging
7590 Administration for Children and Families
7555 Program Support Center

TABLE OF ORGANIZATIONS AND CODES
EXECUTIVE DEPARTMENTS
(and their associated organizations)

Code Organization

7000 **HOMELAND SECURITY**, Department of

7001 Office of the Secretary, Department of Homeland Security
7002 Immediate Office of the Secretary
7003 U.S. Citizenship and Immigration Services
7004 Office of the Inspector General
7008 U.S. Coast Guard
7009 U.S. Secret Service

7012 U.S. Immigration and Customs Enforcement
7013 Transportation Security Administration
7014 U.S. Customs and Border Protection
7015 Federal Law Enforcement Training Center

7022 Federal Emergency Management Agency

7032 Office for Information Analysis
7033 Office for Infrastructure Protection

7040 Under Secretary for Science and Technology
7041 Office of the Under Secretary for Science and Technology

7050 Under Secretary for Management
7051 Office of the Under Secretary for Management

TABLE OF ORGANIZATIONS AND CODES
EXECUTIVE DEPARTMENTS
(and their associated organizations)

Code Organization

8600 **HOUSING AND URBAN DEVELOPMENT**, Department of

8601 Office of the Secretary of Housing and Urban Development
8602   Deputy Secretary of Housing and Urban Development
8613   HUD Board of Contract Appeals
8615   Office of Administrative Law Judges
8617   Office of Small and Disadvantaged Business Utilization
8622   Assistant Deputy Secretary for Field Policy and Management
8656   Office of Federal Housing Enterprise Oversight
8603 Office of General Counsel
8604 Office of Inspector General
8605 Assistant Secretary for Administration
8606 Office of Chief Financial Officer
8607 Assistant Secretary for Congressional and Intergovernmental Relations
8608 Assistant Secretary for Public Affairs
8611 Assistant Secretary for Fair Housing and Equal Opportunity
8620 Assistant Secretary for Community Planning and Development
8630 Assistant Secretary for Housing--Federal Housing Commissioner
8635 Assistant Secretary for Public and Indian Housing
8645 Assistant Secretary for Policy Development and Research
8625 Government National Mortgage Association (Ginnie Mae)
8653 Office of Healthy Homes and Lead Hazard Control
8654 Office of the Chief Procurement Officer
8627 Office of Departmental Equal Employment Opportunity
8651 Office of Departmental Operations and Coordination
8652 Office of the Chief Information Officer
8658 Center for Faith-based and Community Initiatives

TABLE OF ORGANIZATIONS AND CODES
EXECUTIVE DEPARTMENTS
(and their associated organizations)

Code Organization

8600   **HOUSING AND URBAN DEVELOPMENT**, Department of - continued

8659   Office of Field Policy and Management
865A   Office of the Field Policy and Management Region I, Boston Regional Office
865B   Office of the Field Policy and Management Region II, New York Regional Office
865C   Office of the Field Policy and Management Region III, Philadelphia Regional
        Office
865D   Office of Field Policy and Management Region IV, Atlanta Regional Office
865E   Office of Field Policy and Management Region V, Chicago Regional Office
865F   Office of Field Policy and Management Region VI, Fort Worth Regional Office
865G   Office of Field Policy and Management Region VII, Kansas City Regional Office
865H   Office of Field Policy and Management Region VIII, Denver Regional Office
865J   Office of Field Policy and Management Region IX, San Francisco Regional
        Office
865K   Office of Field Policy and Management Region X, Seattle Regional Office

~~Government-Sponsored Enterprise:~~

8681   Federal National Mortgage Association (Fannie Mae)
8683   Federal Home Loan Mortgage Corporation (Freddie Mac)

TABLE OF ORGANIZATIONS AND CODES
EXECUTIVE DEPARTMENTS
(and their associated organizations)

Code Organization

1400   **INTERIOR**, Department of the

140S   Office of the Secretary of the Interior
1402   Office of the Deputy Secretary of the Interior
1406   Office of Policy, Management and Budget/Chief Financial Officer
1413   Office of Hearings and Appeals
1418   Office of Small and Disadvantaged Business Utilization
1410   Office of the Chief Information Officer
1407   Office of Congressional and Legislative Affairs
1408   Office of Communications
1409   Office of Insular Affairs
1411   Office for Equal Opportunity
1414   Executive Secretariat & Office of Regulatory Affairs
1415   Office of the Special Trustee for American Indians

1403   Office of the Solicitor
1404   Office of the Inspector General
1428   National Business Center

142F   Fish and Wildlife and Parks (Assistant Secretary)
1443   National Park Service
1448   U.S. Fish and Wildlife Service

1450   Indian Affairs (Assistant Secretary)

142L   Land and Minerals Management (Assistant Secretary)
1422   Bureau of Land Management
1435   Minerals Management Service
1438   Office of Surface Mining, Reclamation and Enforcement

142W Water and Science (Assistant Secretary)
1425   Bureau of Reclamation
1434 Geological   Survey

TABLE OF ORGANIZATIONS AND CODES
EXECUTIVE DEPARTMENTS
(and their associated organizations)

Code Organization

1400   **INTERIOR**, Department of - continued

~~Associated Federal Organizations:~~

1460   Board on Geographic Names
1464   Illinois and Michigan Canal National Heritage Corridor Commission
1465   Metropolitan River Corridors Study Committee
1461   Migratory Bird Conservation Commission
1469 National   Indian Gaming Commission
1467   Utah Reclamation Mitigation and Conservation Commission
1468   Indian Arts and Crafts Board
1466 Endangered   Species Committee

TABLE OF ORGANIZATIONS AND CODES
EXECUTIVE DEPARTMENTS
(and their associated organizations)

Code Organization

1500 **JUSTICE**, Department of

1501 Offices, Boards and Divisions
(includes the following: Attorney General, Deputy Attorney General, Associate Attorney General, Office of Policy Development, Office of Public Affairs, Office of Legislative Affairs, Office of Legal Counsel, Solicitor General, Criminal Division, Civil Division, Civil Rights Division, Antitrust Division, Tax Division, Environment and Natural Resources Division, Justice Management Division, Office of Professional Responsibility, Office of the Pardon Attorney, U.S. National Central Bureau-INTERPOL, U.S. Parole Commission, Office of Intelligence Policy and Review, Foreign Claims Settlement Commission, Office of Information and Privacy, and Community Oriented Policing Services)

1504 Office of the Inspector General
1524 Drug Enforcement Administration
1526 Executive Office for U.S. Attorneys and the Offices of U.S. Attorneys
1528 Immigration and Naturalization Service
1530 Executive Office for Immigration Review
1535 Community Relations Service
1540 Bureau of Prisoners/Federal Prison System
1544 U.S. Marshals Service
1549 Federal Bureau of Investigation
1550 Office of Justice Programs
(includes the following: Bureau of Justice Assistance, Bureau of Justice Statistics, National Institute of Justice, Office for Victims of Crimes, Office of Juvenile Justice and Delinquency Prevention, and Executive Office for Weed and Seed)

1555 Executive Office for U.S. Trustee
1560 Bureau of Alcohol, Tobacco, Firearms and Explosives

TABLE OF ORGANIZATIONS AND CODES
EXECUTIVE DEPARTMENTS
(and their associated organizations)

Code Organization

1600   **LABOR**, Department of

160S   Office of the Secretary of Labor
1601   Immediate Office of the Secretary of Labor
160U   Office of the Deputy Secretary of Labor
1610   Office of Adjudicatory Service
1613   Office of Administrative Law Judges
1615   Benefits Review Board
1616   Employees Compensation Appeals Board
1617   Administrative Review Board
1618   Office of Small Business Programs
1619 Executive   Secretariat
1620   Office of 21st Century Workforce
1623   Center for Faith-based and Community Initiatives
1607   Office of the Assistant Secretary of Labor for Congressional and
            Intergovernmental Affairs
1608   Office of Public Affairs
1655 Women's   Bureau
1609   Bureau of International Labor Affairs
1603   Office of the Solicitor
1604   Office of Inspector General
1605   Office of the Assistant Secretary for Administration and Management
1622   Office of the Chief Financial Officer
1606   Office of the Assistant Secretary for Policy
1625   Bureau of Labor Statistics
1631   Office of Job Corps
1630   Employment and Training Administration
1635 Employment   Standards Administration
1645   Mine Safety and Health Administration
1650   Occupational Safety and Health Administration
1621   Employee Benefits Security Administration
1653   Veterans Employment and Training Services
1667   Office of Disability Employment Policy

Associated Federal Organizations:

1665   Pension Benefit Guaranty Corporation

TABLE OF ORGANIZATIONS AND CODES
EXECUTIVE DEPARTMENTS
(and their associated organizations)

Code Organization

1900	**STATE**, Department of
190S	Office of the Secretary of State
1901	Immediate Office of the Secretary of State
1902	Office of the Deputy Secretary of State
1858	Office of U.S. Ambassador to the United Nations
1906	Policy Planning Council
1907	Bureau of Legislative Affairs
1910	Chief of Protocol
1911	Office of Equal Employment Opportunity and Civil Rights
1912	Coordinator for Counter-Terrorism
1917	Executive Secretary
1904	Office of the Inspector General
1939	Bureau of Intelligence and Research
1903	Office of the Legal Adviser
1916	Counselor of the Department
1918	Chief of Staff
1905	Office of the Under Secretary for Management
1930	Bureau of Consular Affairs
1931	Chief Financial Officer
1932	Foreign Service Institute
1935	Director General of the Foreign Service and Director of Human Resource
1937	Bureau of Administration
1938	Bureau of Diplomatic Security and Office of Foreign Missions
1943	Office of Information Resources Management
1934	Bureau of Overseas Buildings Operations
1946	Bureau of Resource Management
1913	Office of the Under Secretary for Political Affairs
1921	Bureau of African Affairs
1923	Bureau of East Asian and Pacific Affairs
1925	Bureau of European and Eurasian Affairs
1927	Bureau of Western Hemisphere Affairs
1928	Bureau of South Asian Affairs
1929	Bureau of Near Eastern Affairs
1945	Bureau of International Organization Affairs

TABLE OF ORGANIZATIONS AND CODES
EXECUTIVE DEPARTMENTS
(and their associated organizations)

Code Organization

1900 **STATE**, Department of - continued

1914 Office of the Under Secretary for Economic and Agricultural Affairs
1933   Bureau of Economic and Business Affair
1934   Bureau of Overseas Buildings Operations

1915 Office of the Under Secretary for Arms Control and
    International Security Affairs
1950   Bureau of Political-Military Affairs
1951   Assistant Secretary for Arms Control
1955   Assistant Secretary for Non-Proliferation
1956   Assistant Secretary for Verification and Compliance

19TB Office of the Under Secretary for Public Diplomacy and Public Affairs
1952   Bureau of Public Affairs
1953   Bureau of Educational and Cultural Affairs
1957   International Public Information Core Group Secretariat
1959   Office of International Information Programs

1941 Office of the Under Secretary for Global Affairs
1936   Bureau of Democracy, Human Rights and Labor
1942   Bureau of International Narcotics and Law Enforcement Affairs
1948   Bureau of Oceans and International Environmental and Scientific Affairs
1954   Bureau of Population, Refugees and Migration

    Associated Federal Organization:

1960 Artistic Ambassador Advisory Committee
1961 Board of Foreign Scholarships
1962 Cultural Property Advisory Committee
1963. U.S. Advisory Commission on Public Diplomacy
1964 J. William Fulbright Foreign Scholarship Board
1965 Center for Cultural and Technical Interchange between East and West
1966 Eastern Europe Student Exchange Program
1967 Center for Cultural and Technical Interchange between North and South
1968 Russian Far East Technical Assistance Center
1969 National Endowment for Democracy
195A Eisenhower Exchange Fellowship Program
195B Israeli Arab Scholarship Program

TABLE OF ORGANIZATIONS AND CODES
EXECUTIVE DEPARTMENTS
(and their associated organizations)

Code Organization

1900 **STATE**, Department of –continued

Associated Federal Organization -continued:

195C   Broadcasting Board of Governors
19BC   U.S. and Canada International Boundary Commission
19BJ   U.S. and Canada International Joint Commission
19BM   U.S. and Mexico International Boundary and Water Commission
19BE   U.S. and Canada Border Environment Cooperation Commission

NOTE: Agencies (19BC-19BE) are listed under International Organizations, this secondary listing is for user convenience only.

Federally Aided Organizations:

1991   American Institute in Taiwan
1993   Asia Foundation

TABLE OF ORGANIZATIONS AND CODES
EXECUTIVE DEPARTMENTS
(and their associated organizations)

Code Organization

6900   **TRANSPORTATION**, Department of

690S   Office of the Secretary of Transportation
6901   Immediate Office of the Secretary of Transportation
6917   Deputy Secretary of Transportation
6902   Associate Deputy Secretary/Office of Intermodalism
6916   Office of Drug and Alcohol Policy and Compliance
6903   Office of General Counsel
6905   Assistant   Secretary for Administration
6906   Assistant Secretary for Budget and Programs/Chief Financial Officer
6907   Assistant Secretary for Governmental Affairs
6908   Assistant Secretary - Office of Public Affairs
6909   Assistant Secretary for Transportation Policy
6911   Office of Civil Rights
6912   Board of Contract Appeals
6914   Executive   Secretariat
6915   Office of Intelligence, Security and Emergency Response
6918   Office of Small and Disadvantaged Business Utilization
          Business Resources Center
6910   Office of the Chief Information Officer
6922   Assistant Secretary for Aviation and International Affairs

6904   Office of Inspector General

6920   Federal Aviation Administration
6913   Office of Commercial Space Transportation

6925   Federal Highway Administration
6930   Federal Railroad Administration
6938   Maritime   Administration
6940   National Highway Traffic Safety Administration
6943   Research and Innovative Technology Administration
6947   Saint Lawrence Seaway Development Corporation
6953   Federal Motor Carrier Safety Administration
6955   Federal Transit Administration
6957   Pipeline and Hazardous Materials Safety Administration

TABLE OF ORGANIZATIONS AND CODES
EXECUTIVE DEPARTMENTS
(and their associated organizations)

Code Organization

6900 **TRANSPORTATION**, Department of - continued
~~Associated Federal Organizations:~~

6959 Surface   Transportation Board
       NOTE: This agency was formerly the Interstate Commerce Commission, which had been assigned code 3000.

~~Federally Aided Organization:~~

6991   National Railroad Passenger Corporation (AMTRAK)

TABLE OF ORGANIZATIONS AND CODES
EXECUTIVE DEPARTMENTS
(and their associated organizations)

Code Organization

2000   **TREASURY**, Department of the

2001 Departmental   Offices
2004 Inspector   General
2014   Office of the Inspector General for Tax Administration
2033   Financial Management Service
2036   Bureau of the Public Debt
2046   Office of the Comptroller of the Currency
2047   Office of Thrift Supervision
2041   Bureau of Engraving and Printing
2044   United States Mint
2022   Alcohol and Tobacco Tax and Trade Bureau
2026   Financial Crimes Enforcement Network
2050   Internal Revenue Service

Associated Federal Organizations:

2061   Federal Financing Bank
2066   Community Development Financial Institutions

Federally Aided Organizations:

2093   District of Columbia

TABLE OF ORGANIZATIONS AND CODES
EXECUTIVE DEPARTMENTS
(and their associated organizations)

Code Organization

3600 **VETERANS AFFAIRS**, Department of

    3601   Office of the Secretary
    3602   Office of the Deputy Secretary
    3615   Center for Minority Veterans
    3616 Center   for Women Veterans
    3617   Office of Employment Discrimination Complaint Adjudication
    3619   Chief of Staff
    3618   Special Assistant for Veterans Service Organization Liaison

    3603 General   Counsel
    3604 Inspector   General
    3610   Board of Veterans Appeals
    3612   Board of Contract Appeals
    3613   Office of Small and Disadvantaged Business Utilization
    3620   Under Secretary for Health / Veterans Health Administration
    3630   Under Secretary for Memorial Affairs/National Cemetery System
    3640   Under Secretary for Benefits / Veterans Benefit Administration

    3605   Assistant Secretary for Management
    3628   Immediate Office of Assistant Secretary for Management
    3625   Deputy Assistant Secretary for Budget
    3627   Deputy Assistant Secretary for Financial Management
    3643   Deputy Assistant Secretary for Acquisition and Materiel Management
    3644   Director – Asset Enterprise Management

    3606   Assistant Secretary for Policy and Planning
    3624   Immediate Office of Assistance Secretary for Policy and Planning
    3622   Deputy Assistant Secretary for Policy
    3623   Deputy Assistant Secretary for Planning and Evaluation
    3655   Deputy Assistant Secretary for Security Preparedness
    3656   Deputy Assistant Secretary for Security and Law Enforcement

    3607   Assistant Secretary for Public and Intergovernmental Affairs
    3636   Immediate Office of Assistance Secretary for Public and
                Intergovernmental Affairs

TABLE OF ORGANIZATIONS AND CODES
EXECUTIVE DEPARTMENTS
(and their associated organizations)

Code Organization

3600 VETERANS   AFFAIRS, Department of - continued

3637   Deputy Assistant Secretary for Intergovernmental Affairs and International Affairs

3638   Deputy Assistant Secretary for Public Affairs

3608   Assistant Secretary for Congressional and Legislative Affairs

3646   Immediate Office of Assistant Secretary for Congressional Affairs

3647 Director,   Congressional Affairs

3648   Deputy Assistant Secretary for Legislative Affairs

3611   Assistant Secretary for Human Resources and Administration

3649   Immediate Office of Assistant Secretary for
              Human Resources and Administration

3632   Deputy Assistant Secretary for Diversity and Equal Employment Opportunity

3633   Director – Office of Administration

3634   Deputy Assistant Secretary for Human Resources Management and Labor Relations

3641   Deputy Assistant Secretary for Office of Resolution Management

3645   Associate Deputy for Labor - Management Relations

3650   Assistant Secretary for Information and Technology

3651   Immediate Office of the Assist. Sec. for Information & Technology

3652   Deputy Assistant Sec. For Information & Technology

3621   Director, Austin Automation Center

TABLE OF ORGANIZATIONS AND CODES
OTHER INDEPENDENT FEDERAL AGENCIES, BOARDS, COMMISSIONS, COUNCILS, FOUNDATIONS, OFFICES, QUASI-FEDERAL ORGANIZATIONS AND FEDERAL-STATE ORGANIZATIONS
(and their associated organizations)

Code Organization

9530   Advisory Council On Historic Preservation

1141   African Development Foundation

7200   U.S. Agency for International Development

7400   American Battle Monuments Commission

4602   Appalachian Regional Commission

9532   Architectural and Transportation Barriers Compliance Board

4965   Arctic Research Commission

84AF   Armed Forces Retirement Home
97NH   United States Naval Home
8400   United States Soldiers' and Airmen's Home

9560   Barry Goldwater Scholarship and Excellence in Education Foundation

9568   Broadcasting Board of Governors

9522   Centennial of Flight Commission

5600 Central   Intelligence Agency

9565   Chemical Safety and Hazard Investigation Board

7635   Christopher Columbus Fellowship Foundation

9567   Commission for the Preservation of America's Heritage Abroad

9537   Commission of Fine Arts

9517   Commission on Civil Rights

TABLE OF ORGANIZATIONS AND CODES
OTHER INDEPENDENT FEDERAL AGENCIES, BOARDS, COMMISSIONS, COUNCILS, FOUNDATIONS, OFFICES, QUASI-FEDERAL ORGANIZATIONS AND FEDERAL-STATE ORGANIZATIONS
(and their associated organizations)

Code Organization

4836   Commission on Executive, Legislative and Judicial Salaries

9518   Committee for Purchase from People who are Blind or Severely Disabled

9507   Commodity Futures Trading Commission

6100   Consumer Product Safety Commission

9577 Corporation   for National and Community Service

2092   Corporation for Public Broadcasting

9594   Court Services and Offender Supervision Agency for the District of Columbia
959D   Office of the Director – CSOSA
955P   Pretrial Services Agency - CSOSA

9516   Defense Nuclear Facilities Safety Board

9547   Delta Regional Authority

9572   Denali Commission

9523   Election Assistance Commission

TABLE OF ORGANIZATIONS AND CODES
OTHER INDEPENDENT FEDERAL AGENCIES, BOARDS, COMMISSIONS, COUNCILS, FOUNDATIONS, OFFICES, QUASI-FEDERAL ORGANIZATIONS AND FEDERAL-STATE ORGANIZATIONS
(and their associated organizations)

Code Organization

Code	Organization
6800	**ENVIRONMENTAL PROTECTION AGENCY**
680S	Office of the Administrator of EPA
6801	Immediate Office of the Administrator of EPA
6802	Deputy Administrator
68SA	Associate Administrator for Office of Public Affairs
68SB	Associate Administrator for Congressional and Intergovernmental Relations
68SC	Office of Homeland Security
68SD	Environmental Appeals Board
68SE	Executive Secretariat
68SF	Office of Executive Services
68SG	Office of Administrative Law Judges
68SH	Office of Civil Rights
68SJ	Office of Cooperative Environmental Management
68SK	Office of Small and Disadvantaged Business Utilization
68SL	Office of Policy, Economics and Innovation
68SM	Science Advisory Board
68SN	Office of Environmental Education
68SO	Office of Children's Health Protection
6803	Office of General Counsel
6804	Office of the Inspector General
6805	Assistant Administrator for Administration and Resources Management
6809	Assistant Administrator for International Affairs
6820	Assistant Administrator for Air and Radiation
6825	Assistant Administrator for Enforcement and Compliance Assurance
6830	Assistant Administrator for Prevention, Pesticides, and Toxic Substances
6840	Assistant Administrator for Research and Development
6845	Assistant Administrator for Water
6850	Assistant Administrator for Solid Waste and Emergency Response
6860	Assistant Administrator for Environmental Information
6853	Office of the Chief Financial Officer

TABLE OF ORGANIZATIONS AND CODES
OTHER INDEPENDENT FEDERAL AGENCIES, BOARDS, COMMISSIONS, COUNCILS, FOUNDATIONS, OFFICES, QUASI-FEDERAL ORGANIZATIONS AND FEDERAL-STATE ORGANIZATIONS
(and their associated organizations)

Code Organization

Associated Federal Organization:

4500   Equal Employment Opportunity Commission

4567   Interagency Committee on Employment of People with Disabilities

8300   Export-Import Bank of the U.S.

7800 Farm   Credit Administration

Government-Sponsored Enterprises:

7881   Bank for Cooperatives
7884   Farm Credit Banks
7886   Farm Credit System Financial Assistance Corporation
7888   Farm Credit System Insurance Corporation
7889   Federal Agricultural Mortgage Corporation (Farmer Mac)

TBD   Federal Accounting Standards Advisory Board

2700   Federal Communications Commission

5100   Federal Deposit Insurance Corporation

9506   Federal Election Commission

TABLE OF ORGANIZATIONS AND CODES
OTHER INDEPENDENT FEDERAL AGENCIES, BOARDS, COMMISSIONS, COUNCILS, FOUNDATIONS, OFFICES, QUASI-FEDERAL ORGANIZATIONS AND FEDERAL-STATE ORGANIZATIONS
(and their associated organizations)

Code Organization

9562 Federal   Financial Institutions Examination Council

9540   Federal Housing Finance Board

~~Government-Sponsored Enterprise~~

95HL   Federal Home Loan Banks
9585   Financing Corporation (FICO)

5400   Federal Labor Relations Authority

6500   Federal Maritime Commission

9300   Federal Mediation and Conciliation Service

9504   Federal Mine Safety and Health Review Commission

9559   Federal Reserve System, Board of Governors

2600   Federal Retirement Thrift Investment Board

2900   Federal Trade Commission

TABLE OF ORGANIZATIONS AND CODES
OTHER INDEPENDENT FEDERAL AGENCIES, BOARDS, COMMISSIONS, COUNCILS, FOUNDATIONS, OFFICES, QUASI-FEDERAL ORGANIZATIONS AND FEDERAL-STATE ORGANIZATIONS
(and their associated organizations)

Code Organization

4700   **GENERAL SERVICES ADMINISTRATION**

4701   Immediate Office of the Administrator
4704   Office of Inspector General
4712   GSA Board of Contract Appeals
4703   Office of General Counsel
4705   Office of the Chief People Officer
4707   Office of Congressional and Intergovernmental Affairs
4708   Office of Citizen Services and Communications
4717   Office of the Chief Financial Officer
4722   Offices of the Regional Administrators
4724   Office of Civil Rights
4728   Office of Small Business Utilization
4732   Office of the Federal Acquisition Service
4740   Public Buildings Service
4745   Office of Governmentwide Policy
4750   Office of the Chief Information Officer
4743   Office of Childcare
4760   Office of the Chief Acquisition Officer

TABLE OF ORGANIZATIONS AND CODES
OTHER INDEPENDENT FEDERAL AGENCIES, BOARDS, COMMISSIONS, COUNCILS, FOUNDATIONS, OFFICES, QUASI-FEDERAL ORGANIZATIONS AND FEDERAL-STATE ORGANIZATIONS
(and their associated organizations)

Code Organization

9510   Harry S. Truman Scholarship Foundation

9535   Institute of American Indian and Alaska Native Culture and Arts Development

9554   Interagency Council on the Homeless

1143 Inter-American   Foundation

4607   Interstate Commission on the Potomac River Basin

9541   James Madison Memorial Fellowship Foundation

9512 Japan-U.S.   Friendship Commission

2095   Legal Services Corporation

9513 Marine Mammal   Commission

4100   Merit Systems Protection Board

9543   Millennium Challenge Corporation

9545   Morris K. Udall Scholarship and Excellence in National Environmental Policy Foundation

TABLE OF ORGANIZATIONS AND CODES
OTHER INDEPENDENT FEDERAL AGENCIES, BOARDS, COMMISSIONS, COUNCILS, FOUNDATIONS, OFFICES, QUASI-FEDERAL ORGANIZATIONS AND FEDERAL-STATE ORGANIZATIONS
(and their associated organizations)

Code Organization

8000   **NATIONAL AERONAUTICS AND SPACE ADMINISTRATION**

8001 Headquarters,   NASA
8020   Ames Research Center
8044   George C. Marshall Space Flight Center
8026   Goddard Space Flight Center
8035   John F. Kennedy Space Center
8038   Langley Research Center
8041   John H. Glenn Research Center at Lewis Field
8032   Lyndon B. Johnson Space Center
8047   John C. Stennis Space Center
8025   NASA Shared Services Center
8022   Dryden Flight Research Center
8029   NASA Management Office, Jet Propulsion Laboratory

TABLE OF ORGANIZATIONS AND CODES
OTHER INDEPENDENT FEDERAL AGENCIES, BOARDS, COMMISSIONS, COUNCILS, FOUNDATIONS, OFFICES, QUASI-FEDERAL ORGANIZATIONS AND FEDERAL-STATE ORGANIZATIONS
(and their associated organizations)

Code Organization

8800 **NATIONAL ARCHIVES AND RECORDS ADMINISTRATION**

Associated Federal Organizations:

8852 Information Security Oversight Office
8861 National Archives Trust Fund Board
8862 National Historical Publications and Records Commission
8865 Administrative Committee of the Federal Register

9502 National Capital Planning Commission

9527 National Commission on Libraries and Information Science

9528 Office of the Federal Coordinator Alaska Natural Gas Transportation Projects

9555 National Communications System
9509 National Council on Disability

9525 National Counterintelligence Center

2500 National Credit Union Administration

TABLE OF ORGANIZATIONS AND CODES
OTHER INDEPENDENT FEDERAL AGENCIES, BOARDS, COMMISSIONS, COUNCILS, FOUNDATIONS, OFFICES, QUASI-FEDERAL ORGANIZATIONS AND FEDERAL-STATE ORGANIZATIONS
(and their associated organizations)

Code Organization

5900 NATIONAL FOUNDATION ON THE ARTS AND THE HUMANITIES

5915   Federal Council on the Arts and the Humanities
5950   Institute of Museum Services
5920   National Endowment for the Arts
5940   National Endowment for the Humanities

Associated Federal Organizations:

5963   National Council on the Arts
5966   National Council on the Humanities

6300   National Labor Relations Board

9524 National Mediation   Board

TABLE OF ORGANIZATIONS AND CODES
OTHER INDEPENDENT FEDERAL AGENCIES, BOARDS, COMMISSIONS, COUNCILS, FOUNDATIONS, OFFICES, QUASI-FEDERAL ORGANIZATIONS AND
FEDERAL-STATE ORGANIZATIONS
(and their associated organizations)

Code Organization

4900 NATIONAL   SCIENCE FOUNDATION

~~Associated Federal Organization:~~

4960   National Science Board

9508   National Transportation Safety Board

8291   Neighborhood Reinvestment Corporation

3100   Nuclear Regulatory Commission

4856   Nuclear Waste Technical Review Board

9514   Occupational Safety and Health Review Commission

9549   Office of Government Ethics

4849   Office of Navajo and Hopi Indian Relocation

TABLE OF ORGANIZATIONS AND CODES
OTHER INDEPENDENT FEDERAL AGENCIES, BOARDS, COMMISSIONS, COUNCILS, FOUNDATIONS, OFFICES, QUASI-FEDERAL ORGANIZATIONS AND FEDERAL-STATE ORGANIZATIONS
(and their associated organizations)

Code Organization

2400   OFFICE OF PERSONNEL MANAGEMENT

Associated Federal Organizations:
2460   Federal Prevailing Rate Advisory Committee
2461   President's Commission on White House Fellowships

Federal Executive Boards (FEB)
24P1   Federal Executive Board-Albuquerque, NM
24P4   Federal Executive Board-Atlanta, GA
24P7   Federal Executive Board-Baltimore, MD
24Q1   Federal Executive Board-Boston, MA
24Q4   Federal Executive Board-Buffalo, NY
24Q7   Federal Executive Board-Chicago, IL
24R1   Federal Executive Board-Cincinnati, OH
24R4   Federal Executive Board-Cleveland, OH
24R7   Federal Executive Board-Dallas-Ft.Worth, TX
24S1   Federal Executive Board-Denver, CO
24S4   Federal Executive Board-Detroit, MI
24S7   Federal Executive Board-Honolulu, HI
24T1   Federal Executive Board-Houston, TX
24T4   Federal Executive Board-Kansas City, KS
24T7   Federal Executive Board-Los Angeles, CA
24V1   Federal Executive Board-Miami, FL
24V4   Federal Executive Board-Newark, NJ
24V7   Federal Executive Board-New Orleans, LA
24W1 Federal Executive Board-New York City, NY
24W4 Federal Executive Board-Oklahoma, City, OK
24W7 Federal Executive Board-Philadelphia, PA
24X1   Federal Executive Board-Pittsburgh, PA
24X4   Federal Executive Board-Portland, OR
24X7   Federal Executive Board-St. Louis, MO
24Y1   Federal Executive Board-San Antonio, TX
24Y4   Federal Executive Board-San Francisco, CA
24Y7   Federal Executive Board-Seattle, WA
24Z1   Federal Executive Board-Twin Cities, MN

TABLE OF ORGANIZATIONS AND CODES
OTHER INDEPENDENT FEDERAL AGENCIES, BOARDS,
COMMISSIONS, COUNCILS, FOUNDATIONS, OFFICES,
QUASI-FEDERAL ORGANIZATIONS AND
FEDERAL-STATE ORGANIZATIONS
(and their associated organizations)

Code Organization

6201   Office of Special Counsel

7100   Overseas Private Investment Corporation

1145 Peace   Corps

9570 Presidio   Trust

6000   Railroad Retirement Board

5000   Securities and Exchange Commission

~~Federally Aided Organization:~~
5094   Securities Investor Protection Corporation

9000   Selective Service System

7300   Small Business Administration

~~Associated Federal Organization~~

7360   National Women's Business Council

3300 Smithsonian   Institution, except units administered under separate Board of Trustees

3320 Smithsonian   Institution, except units administered under separate Boards of Trustees

3352   John F. Kennedy Center for the Performing Arts

3355   National Gallery of Art

3358   Woodrow Wilson International Center for Scholars

TABLE OF ORGANIZATIONS AND CODES
OTHER INDEPENDENT FEDERAL AGENCIES, BOARDS, COMMISSIONS, COUNCILS, FOUNDATIONS, OFFICES, QUASI-FEDERAL ORGANIZATIONS AND
FEDERAL-STATE   ORGANIZATIONS
(and their associated organizations)

Code Organization

2800   **SOCIAL SECURITY ADMINISTRATION**

2801   Office of the Commissioner
2803   Office of the General Counsel
2804   Office of the Inspector General
2814   Office of the Chief Actuary
2805   Deputy Commissioner - Finance, Assessment and Management and Senior Financial Executive
2806   Deputy Commissioner - Programs, Policy, Evaluation, and Communications
2807   Deputy Commissioner - Legislation and Congressional Affairs
2810   Deputy Commissioner - Human Resources
2811   Deputy Commissioner - Systems
2812   Deputy Commissioner - Operations
2816   Deputy Commissioner – Communications
2818   Deputy Commissioner – Disability and Income Security Programs

4817   State Justice Institute

6400 Tennessee   Valley Authority

~~Government Sponsored Enterprise~~

2281   Resolution Funding Corporation (REFCORP)

1153   Trade and Development Agency
       NOTE: This agency was previously a part of the International Development Cooperation Agency. The code has not been changed.

9589   United Mine Workers of America Benefit Funds

9531   United States Holocaust Memorial Museum

TABLE OF ORGANIZATIONS AND CODES
OTHER INDEPENDENT FEDERAL AGENCIES, BOARDS, COMMISSIONS, COUNCILS, FOUNDATIONS, OFFICES, QUASI-FEDERAL ORGANIZATIONS AND FEDERAL-STATE ORGANIZATIONS
(and their associated organizations)

Code Organization

Associated Federal Organizations:

9580   United States Institute of Peace

3400   U.S. International Trade Commission

7200   Agency for International Development
7100   Overseas Private Investment Corporation
1800   U. S. Postal Service
1804   Office of the Inspector General of the U.S. Postal Service
1810   U. S. Postal Inspection Service

Associated Federal Organization:

1861 Postal   Rate Commission
1865   Citizens' Stamp Advisory Committee
9590   Valles Caldera Trust
9591   Vietnam Education Foundation
9574   White House Commission on the National Moment of Remembrance

4608   The Port Authority of NY and NJ
4609 Washington Metropolitan   Area Transit Authority

TABLE OF ORGANIZATIONS AND CODES
OTHER INDEPENDENT FEDERAL AGENCIES, BOARDS, COMMISSIONS, COUNCILS, FOUNDATIONS, OFFICES, QUASI-FEDERAL ORGANIZATIONS AND FEDERAL-STATE ORGANIZATIONS
(and their associated organizations)

Code Organization

INTER-AMERICAN ————————————ORGANIZATIONS

19AN Inter-American Indian Institute
19AA Inter-American Institute for Cooperation on Agriculture
19AS Organization of American States
19AH Pan-American Health Organization
19AG Pan-American Institute of Geography and History
19AR Pan-American Railway Congress Association
18AP Postal Union of the Americas and Spain and Portugal

INTERNATIONAL ———————BOUNDARY COMMISSIONS

19BM International Boundary and Water Commission: U.S.-Mexico
19BC International Boundary Commission: U.S. and Canada
19BJ International Joint Commission: U.S. and Canada
19BE U.S. - Canada Border Environment Cooperation Commission

BILATERAL ———————ORGANIZATIONS

19DM Joint Mexican-United States Defense Commission
19DC Permanent Joint Board on Defense – U.S. & Canada

INTERNATIONAL FISHERIES ORGANIZATIONS

19FR Commission for the Conservation of Antarctic Marine Living Resources
19FG Great Lakes Fishery Commission
19FT Inter-American Tropical Tuna Commission
19FL International Commission for the Conservation of Atlantic Tunas
19FE International Council for the Exploration of the Sea
19FD Pacific Salmon Commission
19FY North Pacific Marine Science Organization
19FK North Pacific Anadromous Fish Commission
19FH International Pacific Halibut Commission
19FW International Whaling Commission
19FA North Atlantic Salmon Conservation Organization
19FN Northwest Atlantic Fisheries Organization

TABLE OF ORGANIZATIONS AND CODES
OTHER INDEPENDENT FEDERAL AGENCIES, BOARDS, COMMISSIONS, COUNCILS, FOUNDATIONS, OFFICES, QUASI-FEDERAL ORGANIZATIONS AND
FEDERAL-STATE　　　　　　　　　ORGANIZATIONS
(and their associated organizations)

Code Organization

MEMORIAL, MIGRATION AND REFUGEE AID ORGANIZATIONS

19ME International Organization for Migration
19MR International Committee of the Red Cross
19MC U.N. Memorial Cemetery Commission

MULTILATERAL　　　　　　　DEVELOPMENT BANKS

11DB　African Development Fund
11DE　Asian Development Bank
11DK European Bank for Reconstruction and Development
11DT　Inter-American Defense Board
11DH Inter-American Development Bank
11DR　International Bank for Reconstruction and Development (World Bank)
11DA International Development Association
11DF　International Finance Corporation
11DG International Fund for Agricultural Development
11DM International Monetary Fund
11DW Multilateral Investment Guarantee Agency
11DN North American Development Bank

REGIONAL　　　　　　　ORGANIZATIONS

19RJ Asia-Pacific　Economic Cooperation
19RC　Colombo Plan Council for Technical Cooperation
19RD　Colombo Plan for Cooperative Economic and Social
　　　　　　Development in Asia and the Pacific
11RF　Multinational Force and Observers
19RA　North Atlantic Assembly
19RN　North Atlantic Treaty Organization
19RE　Organization for Economic Cooperation and Development
19RP　South Pacific Commission

TABLE OF ORGANIZATIONS AND CODES
OTHER INDEPENDENT FEDERAL AGENCIES, BOARDS,
COMMISSIONS, COUNCILS, FOUNDATIONS, OFFICES,
QUASI-FEDERAL ORGANIZATIONS AND
FEDERAL-STATE ORGANIZATIONS
(and their associated organizations)

Code Organization

UNITED NATIONS AND AFFILIATED AGENCIES

19UF   Food and Agriculture Organization
19UE   International Atomic Energy Agency
19UA International Civil Aviation Organization
19UL   International Labor Organization
19UG International Maritime Organization
19UT   International Telecommunication Union
19UN United Nations (and special programs)
19UK United Nations Industrial Development Organization
19UP   Universal Postal Union
19UH World Health Organization
19UW World Intellectual Property Organization
19UM World Meteorological Organization

TABLE OF ORGANIZATIONS AND CODES
OTHER INDEPENDENT FEDERAL AGENCIES, BOARDS, COMMISSIONS, COUNCILS, FOUNDATIONS, OFFICES, QUASI-FEDERAL ORGANIZATIONS AND FEDERAL-STATE ORGANIZATIONS
(and their associated organizations)

Code Organization

WORLD   ORGANIZATIONS, Other

Commodity-Oriented

19CF   International Coffee Organization
19CU   International Copper Study Group
19CC   International Cotton Advisory Committee
12CN   International Institute for Cotton
19CJ   International Jute Organization
19CL   International Lead and Zinc Study Group
19CB   International Natural Rubber Organization
19CV   International Office of the Vine and Wine
19CR   International Rubber Study Group
19CS   International Sugar Organization
19CX   International Tropical Timber Organization
19CW International Wheat Council

Experimentation, Measurement, Research, and Study

19EC   International Agency for Research on Cancer
19EM International Bureau of Weights and Measures
19EP   International Center for the Study of the Preservation and
          Restoration of Cultural Property
19EZ   International Office of Epizootics
19ES International   Seed Testing Association
19EV   International Union for the Protection of New Varieties of Plants

Interparliamentary Organizations

19PC   Canada-United States Interparliamentary Group
19PU Interparliamentary Union
19PM Mexico-United States Interparliamentary Group

TABLE OF ORGANIZATIONS AND CODES
OTHER INDEPENDENT FEDERAL AGENCIES, BOARDS, COMMISSIONS, COUNCILS, FOUNDATIONS, OFFICES, QUASI-FEDERAL ORGANIZATIONS AND FEDERAL-STATE ORGANIZATIONS
(and their associated organizations)

Code Organization

Law-Oriented

19LH   Hague Conference on Private International Law
19LA   International Bureau of the Permanent Court of Arbitration
20LP International Criminal   Police Organization (INTERPOL)
19LU   International Institute for the Unification of Private Law
19LM International Organization for Legal Metrology

Navigation, Travel Safety

19NH International Hydrographic Organization
96NC Permanent   International Association of Navigation Congresses
96RC Permanent   International Association of Road Congresses

TABLE OF ORGANIZATIONS AND CODES
OTHER INDEPENDENT FEDERAL AGENCIES, BOARDS, COMMISSIONS, COUNCILS, FOUNDATIONS, OFFICES, QUASI-FEDERAL ORGANIZATIONS AND FEDERAL-STATE ORGANIZATIONS
(and their associated organizations)

Code Organization

WORLD ORGANIZATIONS, Other - Continued

Scientific Unions and Councils

49SZ   Committee on Science and Technology for Development
49SO   International Commission on Optics
49SU International Council of Scientific Unions
49SA   International Astronomical Union
49SG   International Geographical Union
49SE International Geological Union
49SM International Mathematical Union
49SV   International Union for Pure and Applied Biophysics
49SQ   International Union for Quaternary Research
49SK   International Union of Biochemistry & Molecular Biology
49SB   International Union of Biological Sciences
49SX   International Union of Crystallography
49SD   International Union of Geodesy and Geophysics
49SW International Union of Microbiological Societies
49SN   International Union of Nutritional Sciences
49SP   International Union of Physiological Sciences
49SS   International Union of Psychological Science
49SC   International Union of Pure and Applied Chemistry
49SF   International Union of Pure and Applied Physics
49SR   International Union of Radio Sciences
49ST   International Union of Theoretical and Applied Mechanics
49SY   Pacific Science Association

Tariffs, Tourism, and Trade

19TX   Bureau of International Expositions
19TC Customs Cooperation Council
19TT   General Agreement on Tariffs and Trade
19TP   International Bureau for the Publication of Customs Tariffs
19TW World Tourism Organization

Table of Organizations and Codes

Part B: Arrangement by Alphanumeric Sequence of Assigned Codes

TABLE OF ORGANIZATIONS AND CODES

Code Organization

0000 **THE LEGISLATIVE BRANCH**
0001 Congress, generally, no additional specification available
0010 Senate,   The
0050 House of Representatives, The
0099 Joint House and Senate Entities
0100 Architect of the Capitol
0300 Library of Congress
0361 Library of Congress Trust Fund Board
0363 Federal Library & Information Center Committee
0400 Government Printing Office
0500 General Accounting Office
0501   Comptroller General of the United States
0559   GAO, except Comptroller General
0800 Congressional Budget Office
0901 Commission on Security and Cooperation in Europe
0902 Botanic   Garden
0904 Office of Compliance
0905 Dwight D. Eisenhower Memorial Commission
0914 John C. Stennis Center for Public Service Training and Development
0915 Advisory   Commission on Electronic Commerce
0916 National Commission on Terrorism
0923 Commission on the People's Republic of China
0929 U.S. Capitol Preservation Commission
0938 Abraham Lincoln Bicentennial Commission
0962 Permanent Committee for the Oliver Wendell Holmes Devise
0973 National Commission on Terrorist Attacks upon the United States
0975 Commission on the Review of the Overseas Military Facility Structure of the United
        States
0977 Antitrust Modernization Commission

1000 **THE JUDICIAL BRANCH**
1001 Supreme Court of the United States
1002 U.S. Courts of Appeals-Judicial Circuits - except the Federal Circuit
1003 U.S. Court of Appeals for the Federal Circuit
1004 U.S. Court of International Trade
1005 U.S. Court of Federal Claims
1012 U.S. District and Territorial Courts
1018 U.S. Judicial Panel on Multidistrict Litigation
1021 Bankruptcy   Courts
1023   Federal Public Defenders
1025 Court   Security

TABLE OF ORGANIZATIONS AND CODES

Code Organization

1027   Administrative Office of the U.S. Courts
1028   Federal Judicial Center
1030   United States Sentencing Commission
1050   Chief Justice of the United States
1051   Associate Justices of the Supreme Court
1059   Supreme Court, except Justices
1060   Judicial Conference of the United States

1100   **EXECUTIVE OFFICE OF THE PRESIDENT**
1101   President of the United States
1102   National Security Council
1103   Office of Management and Budget
1105   Office of Administration
1109   Office of the United States Trade Representative
1110   Office of Policy Development
1112   Office of Science and Technology Policy
1113   Council of Economic Advisors
1117   White House Office
1118   Executive Residence at the White House
1119   Council on Environmental Quality/Office of Environmental Quality
1121   Director, OMB
1127   Office of the National Drug Control Policy
1129   OMB, except Director
1140   President's Council on Sustainable Development
1141   African Development Foundation
1143 Inter-American   Foundation
1145 Peace   Corps
1148   Office of Homeland Security
1153   Trade and Development Agency
1160   Office of the Vice President of the United States
1165   White House Commission on Presidential Scholars
1170   Commission on the Intelligence Capabilities of the United States Regarding Weapons of
       Mass Destruction
11DA International Development Association
11DB   African Development Fund
11DE   Asian Development Bank
11DF   International Finance Corporation
11DG International Fund for Agricultural Development
11DH Inter-American Development Bank
11DK European Bank for Reconstruction and Development
11DM International Monetary Fund

TABLE OF ORGANIZATIONS AND CODES

Code Organization

11DN North American Development Bank
11DR International Bank for Reconstruction and Development (World Bank)
11DT Inter-American Defense Board
11DW Multilateral Investment Guarantee Agency
11RF Multinational Force and Observers

1200 **AGRICULTURE**, Department of
1201 Office of the Secretary of Agriculture
1203 USDA, Office of the General Counsel
1204 Office of the Inspector General
1205 USDA, Office of the Chief Financial Officer
1208 USDA, Office of Communications
1215 USDA, Office of Operations
1260   Commodity Credit Corporation
1261   Rural Telephone Bank
1263   Federal Crop Insurance Corporation
1291   Land grant colleges and Tuskegee Institute
12A0 USDA, Office of Executive Operations
12A2   USDA, Office of Executive Secretariat
12A4   USDA, Homeland Security
12A5   USDA, Office of the Chief Economist
12A6   USDA, Office of Budget and Program Analysis
12A7 USDA, Office of the Chief Information Officer
12A8 USDA, Office of Small and Disadvantaged Business
12A9   USDA, National Appeals Division
12B0 USDA, Assistant Secretary for Administration
12B1 USDA, Office of Security Services
12B2 USDA, Civil Rights
12B3 Property and Procurement Management
12B5 USDA, Office of Human Capital Management
12B6 USDA, Office of the Administrative Law Judge
12B7 USDA, Office of the Judicial Officer
12B8 USDA, Board of Contract Appeals `
12BD USDA, Office of Ethics

12C0 Under Secretary for Natural Resources and Environment
12C2   Forest Service
12C3   Natural Resources Conservation Service
12CN International Institute for Cotton
12D0 Under Secretary for Farm and Foreign Agricultural Services
12D2   Farm Service Agency

TABLE OF ORGANIZATIONS AND CODES

Code Organization

12D3	Foreign Agricultural Service
12D4	Risk Management Agency
12E0	Under Secretary for Rural Development
12E2	Rural Utilities Service
12E3	Rural Housing Service
12E4	Rural Business Cooperative Service
12E6	National Sheep Industry Improvement Center
12F0	Under Secretary for Food, Nutrition, and Consumer Services
12F2	Food and Nutrition Service
12F3	Center for Nutrition Policy and Promotion
12G0	Under Secretary for Food Safety
12G2	Food Safety and Inspection Service
12H0	Under Secretary for Research, Education, and Economics
12H2	Agricultural Research Service
12H3	Cooperative State Research, Education, and Extension Service
12H4	Economic Research Service
12H5	National Agricultural Statistics Service
12J0	Assistant Secretary for Congressional Relations
12J2	USDA, Office of Congressional and Intergovernmental Relations
12K0	Under Secretary for Marketing and Regulatory Programs
12K2	Agricultural Marketing Service
12K3	Animal and Plant Health Inspection Service
12K4	Grain Inspection, Packers and Stockyards Administration
1300	**COMMERCE**, Department of
1301	Office of the Secretary
1303	Office of the General Counsel
1304	Office of the Inspector General
1306	Office - Chief Financial Officer & Assist. Sec'y for Admin.
1314	Economic and Statistics Administration/Under Secretary for Economic Affairs
1315	Chief Economist
1321	Bureau of Economic Analysis
1323	Bureau of the Census
1325	Economic Development Administration/Assistant Secretary for Economic Development
1330	National Oceanic and Atmospheric Administration/Under Secretary for Oceans and Atmosphere
1335	National Telecommunication and Information Administration/Assistant Secretary for Communications and Information
1341	National Institute of Standards and Technology
1342	National Technical Information Service

TABLE OF ORGANIZATIONS AND CODES

Code Organization

1343   Assistant Secretary for Technology Policy
1344   Patent and Trademark Office/Under Secretary for Intellectual Property
1350   International Trade Administration
1351   Under Secretary for Export Administration/Bureau of Industry and Security
1352   Minority Business Development Agency
1359 Technology   Administration/Under Secretary of Technology
1363   Committee for the Implementation of Textile Agreements
1365   Export Administration Review Board

1400   **INTERIOR**, Department of the
1402   Office of the Deputy Secretary of the Interior
1403   Office of the Solicitor
1404   Office of the Inspector General
1406   Office of Policy, Management and Budget/Chief Financial Officer
1407   Office of Congressional and Legislative Affairs
1408   Office of Communications
1409   Office of Insular Affairs
1410   Office of The Chief Information Officer
140S   Office of the Secretary of the Interior
1411   Office for Equal Opportunity
1413   Office of Hearings and Appeals
1414   Executive Secretariat & Office of Regulatory Affairs
1415   Office of the Special Trustee for American Indians
1418   Office of Small and Disadvantaged Business Utilization
1422   Bureau of Land Management
1425   Bureau of Reclamation
1428   National Business Center
142F   Fish and Wildlife and Parks (Assistant Secretary)
142L   Land and Minerals Management (Assistant Secretary)
142W Water and Science (Assistant Secretary)
1434   Geological Survey
1435   Minerals Management Service
1438   Office of Surface Mining, Reclamation and Enforcement
1443   National Park Service.
1448   U.S. Fish and Wildlife Service
1450   Indian Affairs (Assistant Secretary)
1460   Board on Geographic Names
1461   Migratory Bird Conservation Commission
1464   Illinois and Michigan Canal National Heritage Corridor Commission
1465   Metropolitan River Corridors Study Committee
1466 Endangered   Species Committee

TABLE OF ORGANIZATIONS AND CODES

Code Organization

1467   Utah Reclamation Mitigation and Conservation Commission
1468   Indian Arts and Crafts Board
1469 National   Indian Gaming Commission

1500   **JUSTICE**, Department of
1501   Offices, Boards and Divisions
1504   Office of the Inspector General
1524   Drug Enforcement Administration
1526   Executive Office for U.S. Attorneys and the Offices of U.S. Attorneys
1528   Immigration and Naturalization Service
1530   Executive Office for Immigration Review
1535   Community Relations Service
1540   Bureau of Prisoners/Federal Prison System
1544   U.S. Marshals Service
1549   Federal Bureau of Investigation
1550   Office of Justice Programs
1555   Executive Office for U.S. Trustees
1560   Bureau of Alcohol, Tobacco, Firearms and Explosives

1600   **LABOR**, Department of
1601   Immediate Office of the Secretary of Labor
1603   Office of the Solicitor
1604   Office of Inspector General
1605   Office of the Assistant Secretary for Administration and Management
1606   Office of the Assistant Secretary for Policy
1607   Office of the Assistant Secretary of Labor for Congressional and Intergovernmental
    Affairs
1608   Office of Public Affairs
1609   Bureau of International Labor Affairs
160S   Office of the Secretary of Labor
160U   Office of the Deputy Secretary of Labor
1610   Office of Adjudicatory Services
1613   Office of Administrative Law Judges
1615   Benefits Review Board
1616   Employees Compensation Appeals Board
1617   Administrative Review Board
1618   Office of Small Business Programs
1631   Office of Job Corps
1619   Executive   Secretariat
1620   Office of 21st Century Workforce

TABLE OF ORGANIZATIONS AND CODES

Code Organization

1621   Employee Benefits Security Administration
1622   Office of the Chief Financial Officer
1623   Center for Faith-based and Community Initiatives

1625   Bureau of Labor Statistics
1630   Employment and Training Administration
1635 Employment   Standards Administration
1645   Mine Safety and Health Administration
1650   Occupational Safety and Health Administration
1653   Veterans Employment and Training Services
1655 Women's   Bureau
1665   Pension Benefit Guaranty Corporation
1667   Office of Disability Employment Policy

1700   **NAVY**, Department of the
1708   Immediate Office of the Secretary of the Navy
1709   Navy Staff Offices
1710   Navy Field Offices
1711   Immediate Office of the Chief of Naval Operations
1712   Navy Secretariat/Staff Offices
1714   Office of Naval Research
1715   Naval Intelligence Command
1718   Naval Medical Command
1719   Naval Air Systems Command
1722   Bureau of Naval Personnel
1723   Naval Supply Systems Command
1724   Naval Sea Systems Command
1725   Naval Facilities Engineering Command
1727   U.S. Marine Corps
1730   Special Projects Office
1733   Military Sealift Command
1739   Naval Space and Warfare Systems Command
1741   Naval Systems Management Activity
1752   Commander, Navy Installations
1760   U.S. Atlantic Fleet, Commander In Chief
1761   U.S. Naval Forces, Europe
1762   Chief of Naval Education and Training
1763   Naval Network Operations Command
1765   Naval Oceanography Command
1769   Naval Security Group Command
1770   U.S. Pacific Fleet, Commander in Chief

TABLE OF ORGANIZATIONS AND CODES

Code Organization

1772	Naval Reserve Force
1774	Naval Special Warfare Command
1776	Naval Education and Training Command
17ZS	U.S. Special Operations Command (Navy)

1800	**U.S. POSTAL SERVICE**
1804	Office -Inspector General of the U.S. Postal Service
1810	U.S. Postal Inspection Service
1861	Postal Rate Commission
1865	Citizens' Stamp Advisory Committee
18AP	Postal Union of the Americas and Spain and Portugal

1900	**STATE**, Department of
1901	Immediate Office of the Secretary of State
1902	Office of the Deputy Secretary of State
1903	Office of the Legal Adviser
1904	Office of the Inspector General
1905	Office of the Under Secretary for Management
1906	Policy Planning Council
1907	Bureau of Legislative Affairs
190S	Office of the Secretary of State
1910	Chief of Protocol
1911	Office of Equal Employment Opportunity and Civil Rights
1912	Coordinator for Counter-Terrorism
1913	Office of the Under Secretary for Political Affairs
1914	Office of the Under Secretary for Economic and Agricultural Affairs
1915	Office of the Under Sec'y for Arms Control & Internat'l Security Affairs
1916	Counselor of the Department
1917	Office of Executive Secretary
1918	Chief of Staff

1921	Bureau of African Affairs
1923	Bureau of East Asian and Pacific Affairs
1925	Bureau of European and Eurasian Affairs
1927	Bureau of Western Hemisphere Affairs
1928	Bureau of South Asian Affairs
1929	Bureau of Near Eastern Affairs
1930	Bureau of Consular Affairs
1931	Chief Financial Officer
1932	Foreign Service Institute
1933	Bureau of Economic and Business Affairs

TABLE OF ORGANIZATIONS AND CODES

Code Organization

1935	Director General of the Foreign Service and Director of Human Resource
1936	Bureau of Democracy, Human Rights and Labor
1937	Bureau of Administration
1938	Bureau of Diplomatic Security and Office of Foreign Missions
1939	Bureau of Intelligence and Research
1941	Office of the Under Secretary for Global Affairs
1942	Bureau of International Narcotics and Law Enforcement Affairs
1943	Office of Information Resources Management
1945	Bureau of International Organization Affairs
1946	Bureau of Resource Management
1948	Bureau of Oceans & Internat'l Environmental & Scientific Affairs
1950	Bureau of Political-Military Affairs
1951	Assistant Secretary for Arms Control
1952	Bureau of Public Affairs
1953	Bureau of Educational and Cultural Affairs
1954	Bureau of Population, Refugees and Migration
1955	Assistant Secretary for Non-Proliferation
1956	Assistant Secretary for Verification and Compliance
1957	International Public Information Core Group Secretariat
1959	Office of International Information Programs
195A	Eisenhower Exchange Fellowship Program
1960	Artistic Ambassador Advisory Committee
1961	Board of Foreign Scholarships
1962	Cultural Property Advisory Committee
1963.	U.S. Advisory Commission on Public Diplomacy
1964	J. William Fulbright Foreign Scholarship Board
1965	Center for Cultural and Technical Interchange Between East and West
1966	Eastern Europe Student Exchange Program
1967	Center for Cultural and Technical Interchange Between North and South
1968	Russian Far East Technical Assistance Center
1969	National Endowment for Democracy
195B	Israeli Arab Scholarship Program
195C	Broadcasting Board of Governors
1958	Office of U.S. Ambassador to the United Nations
1959	Office of International Information Programs
1991	American Institute in Taiwan
1993 Asia	Foundation
19AA	Inter-American Institute for Cooperation on Agriculture
19AG	Pan-American Institute of Geography and History
19AH	Pan-American Health Organization
19AN	Inter-American Indian Institute
19AR	Pan-American Railway Congress Association

TABLE OF ORGANIZATIONS AND CODES

Code Organization

19AS   Organization of American States
19BC   U.S. and Canada International Boundary Commission
19BE   U.S. and Canada Border Environment Cooperation Commission
19BJ   U.S. and Canada International Joint Commission
19BM   U.S. and Mexico International Boundary and Water Commission
19CB   International Natural Rubber Organization
19CC   International Cotton Advisory Committee
19CF   International Coffee Organization
19CJ   International Jute Organization
19CL   International Lead and Zinc Study Group
19CR   International Rubber Study Group
19CS   International Sugar Organization
19CU   International Copper Study Group
19CV   International Office of the Vine and Wine
19CW   International Wheat Council
19CX   International Tropical Timber Organization
19DC   Permanent Joint Board on Defense – U.S. & Canada
19DM   Joint Mexican-United States Defense Commission
19EC   International Agency for Research on Cancer
19EM   International Bureau of Weights and Measures
19EP   Internat'l Cntr -- Study of the Preserv. & Restoration of Cultural Property
19ES   International   Seed Testing Association
19EV   International Union for the Protection of New Varieties of Plants
19EZ   International Office of Epizootics
19FA   North Atlantic Salmon Conservation Organization
19FD   Pacific Salmon Commission
19FE   International Council for the Exploration of the Sea
19FG   Great Lakes Fishery Commission
19FH   International Pacific Halibut Commission
19FK   North Pacific Anadromous Fish Commission
19FL   International Commission for the Conservation of Atlantic Tunas
19FN   Northwest Atlantic Fisheries Organization
19FR   Commission for the Conservation of Antarctic Marine Living Resources
19FT   Inter-American Tropical Tuna Commission
19FW   International Whaling Commission
19FY   North Pacific Marine Science Organization
19LA   International Bureau of the Permanent Court of Arbitration
19LH   Hague Conference on Private International Law
19LM   International Organization for Legal Metrology
19LU   International Institute for the Unification of Private Law
19MC   U.N. Memorial Cemetery Commission
19ME   International Organization for Migration

TABLE OF ORGANIZATIONS AND CODES

Code Organization

19MR International Committee of the Red Cross
19NH International Hydrographic Organization
19PC   Canada-United States Interparliamentary Group
19PM Mexico-United States Interparliamentary Group
19PU Interparliamentary Union
19RA   North Atlantic Assembly
19RC   Colombo Plan Council for Technical Cooperation
19RD   Colombo Plan for Coop. Econ. & Social Develop. in Asia and the Pacific
19RE   Organization for Economic Cooperation and Development
19RJ Asia-Pacific   Economic Cooperation
19RN   North Atlantic Treaty Organization
19RP   South Pacific Commission
19TC Customs Cooperation Council
19TP   International Bureau for the Publication of Customs Tariffs
19TT   General Agreement on Tariffs and Trade
19TW World Tourism Organization
19TX   Bureau of International Expositions
19UA International Civil Aviation Organization
19UE   International Atomic Energy Agency
19UF   Food and Agriculture Organization
19UG International Maritime Organization
19UH World Health Organization
19UK United Nations Industrial Development Organization
19UL   International Labor Organization
19UM World Meteorological Organization
19UN United Nations (and special programs)
19UP   Universal Postal Union
19UT   International Telecommunication Union
19UW World Intellectual Property Organization

2000   **TREASURY**, Department of the
2001 Departmental   Offices
2004 Inspector   General
2014   Office of the Inspector General for Tax Administration

2022   Alcohol and Tobacco Tax and Trade Bureau
2026   Financial Crimes Enforcement Network
2033   Financial Management Service
2036   Bureau of the Public Debt
2041   Bureau of Engraving and Printing
2044   United States Mint
2046   Office of the Comptroller of the Currency

TABLE OF ORGANIZATIONS AND CODES

Code Organization

2047	Office of Thrift Supervision
2050	Internal Revenue Service
2061	Federal Financing Bank
2066	Community Development Financial Institutions
2092	Corporation for Public Broadcasting
2093	District of Columbia
2095	Legal Services Corporation
20LP	International Criminal Police Organization (INTERPOL)

2100	**ARMY**, Dept. of the (except Corps of Engineers Civil program financing)
2130	National Guard Bureau
21AE	Acquisition Executive Support Command Agency
21AS	U.S. Army Intelligence and Security Command
21AT	U.S. Army Test and Evaluation Command
21AU	U.S. Army Audit Agency
21BA	U.S. Army Installation Management Agency
21CB	U.S. Army Criminal Investigation Command
21CE	U.S. Army Corps of Engineers, except civil program financing
21CS	Immediate Office of the Chief of Staff of the Army
21CZ	U.S. Army Information Systems Command
21E1	Immed. Office – Comm.-In-Chief - U.S. Army Europe & 7th Army
21E2	21st Theater Army Area Command
21E3	U.S. Army Southern European Task Force
21E5	U.S. Army V Corps
21EB	1st Personnel Command
21ED	U.S. Military Community Activity, Heidelberg
21EN	Seventh Army Training Command
21EO	59th Ordnance Brigade
21FC	U.S. Army Forces Command
21FL	U.S. Army South Command
21G6	U.S. Army Network Enterprise Technology Command/9th Army Signal Command
21GB	Office of the Chief of the National Guard Bureau
21HR	U.S. Army Reserve Command
21HS	U.S. Army Health Services Command
21J1	U.S. Army Element SHAPE
21JA	Joint Activities
21MA	U.S. Military Academy
21MC	U.S. Army Medical Command
21MD	Surgeon General
21MP	U.S. Army Human Resources Command

TABLE OF ORGANIZATIONS AND CODES

Code Organization

21MT	Military Traffic Management Command
21MW	U.S. Army Military District of Washington
21NG	Army National Guard Units (Title 32)
21P1	U.S. Army, Pacific
21P8	Eighth U.S. Army
21PC	Military Entrance Processing Command
21RC	U.S. Army Recruiting Command
21SA	Office of the Secretary of the Army
21SB	Field Operating Offices of the Office of the Secretary of the Army
21SC	U.S. Army Space and Strategic Defense Command
21SE	Field Operating Agencies of the Army Staff Resourced through OA-22
21SF	Field Operating Agencies of the Army Staff
21SJ	Joint Services & Activities Supported by the Office, Sec'y of the Army
21SP	U.S. Special Operation Command (Army)
21SS	Staff Support Agencies of the Chief of Staff, Army
21SU	U.S. Army Southern Command
21TC	U.S. Army Training and Doctrine Command
21X1	U.S. Army Materiel Command (AMC)
21X2	Headquarters, Army Materiel Command
21X3	Headquarters, Staff Support Activities, AMC
21X4	Training Activities, AMC
21X5	U.S. Army Materiel Command, all others
21X6	U.S. Army Missile Command
21X7	U.S. Army Tank-Auto. & Armament Command (TACOM)
21X8	U.S. Army Communications Electronics Command
21X9	U.S.A. Simulation, Training & Instrumentation Command
21XA	U.S. Army Chemical And Biological Defense Command
21XB	U.S. Army Chemical Materials Command
21XC	U.S. Army Soldiers System Command (SSC)
21XD	U.S. Army Research Laboratory Command
21XK	Materiel Acquisition Activities
21XL	Materiel Acquisition Project Managers
21XP	U.S. Army Security Assistance Command
21XQ	U.S. Army Operations Support Command
21XR	U.S. Army Research, Development and Engineering Command
21XT	U.S. Army Test, Measure, & Diagnostic Equip. Activity
21XX	Materiel Readiness Activities
2281	Resolution Funding Corporation (REFCORP)
2300	U.S. Tax Court

TABLE OF ORGANIZATIONS AND CODES

Code Organization

2400	OFFICE OF PERSONNEL MANAGEMENT
2460	Federal Prevailing Rate Advisory Committee
2461	President's Commission on White House Fellowships
24P1	Federal Executive Board-Albuquerque, NM
24P4	Federal Executive Board-Atlanta, GA
24P7	Federal Executive Board-Baltimore, MD
24Q1	Federal Executive Board-Boston, MA
24Q4	Federal Executive Board-Buffalo, NY
24Q7	Federal Executive Board-Chicago, IL
24R1	Federal Executive Board-Cincinnati, OH
24R4	Federal Executive Board-Cleveland, OH
24R7	Federal Executive Board-Dallas-Ft.Worth, TX
24S1	Federal Executive Board-Denver, CO
24S4	Federal Executive Board-Detroit, MI
24S7	Federal Executive Board-Honolulu, HI
24T1	Federal Executive Board-Houston, TX
24T4	Federal Executive Board-Kansas City, KS
24T7	Federal Executive Board-Los Angeles, CA
24V1	Federal Executive Board-Miami, FL
24V4	Federal Executive Board-Newark, NJ
24V7	Federal Executive Board-New Orleans, LA
24W1	Federal Executive Board-New York City, NY
24W4	Federal Executive Board-Oklahoma, City, OK
24W7	Federal Executive Board-Philadelphia, PA
24X1	Federal Executive Board-Pittsburgh, PA
24X4	Federal Executive Board-Portland, OR
24X7	Federal Executive Board-St. Louis, MO
24Y1	Federal Executive Board-San Antonio, TX
24Y4	Federal Executive Board-San Francisco, CA
24Y7	Federal Executive Board-Seattle, WA
24Z1	Federal Executive Board-Twin Cities, MN
2500	National Credit Union Administration
2600	Federal Retirement Thrift Investment Board
2700	Federal Communications Commission
2800	**SOCIAL SECURITY ADMINISTRATION**
2801	Office of the Commissioner
2803	Office of the General Counsel
2804	Office of the Inspector General

TABLE OF ORGANIZATIONS AND CODES

Code Organization

2805	Dep. Comm. – Fin., Assessment & Mgmt. & Senior Fin. Exec.
2806	Deputy Comm. - Programs, Policy, Evaluation, & Commun.
2807	Deputy Commissioner - Legislation and Congressional Affairs
2810	Deputy Commissioner - Human Resources
2811	Deputy Commissioner - Systems
2812	Deputy Commissioner - Operations
2814	Office of the Chief Actuary
2816	Deputy Commissioner - Communications
2818	Deputy Commissioner – Disability and Income Security Programs

2900   Federal Trade Commission

3100   Nuclear Regulatory Commission

3300 Smithsonian   Institution
3320   Smithsonian Institution, except units admin under separate Bds of Trustees
3352   John F. Kennedy Center for the Performing Arts
3355   National Gallery of Art
3358   Woodrow Wilson International Center for Scholars

3400   U.S. International Trade Commission

3600   **VETERANS AFFAIRS**, Department of
3601   Office of the Secretary
3602   Office of the Deputy Secretary
3603 General   Counsel
3604 Inspector   General
3605   Assistant Secretary for Management
3606   Assistant Secretary for Policy and Planning
3607   Assistant Secretary for Public and Intergovernmental Affairs
3608   Assistant Secretary for Congressional and Legislative Affairs
3610   Board of Veterans Appeals
3611   Assistant Secretary for Human Resources and Administration
3612   Board of Contract Appeals
3613   Office of Small and Disadvantaged Business Utilization
3615   Center for Minority Veterans
3616   Center for Women Veterans
3617   Office of Employment Discrimination Complaint Adjudication
3618   Special Assistant for Veterans Service Organization Liaison
3619   Chief of Staff

TABLE OF ORGANIZATIONS AND CODES

Code Organization

3620	Under Secretary for Health / Veterans Health Administration
3621	Director, Austin Automation Center
3622	Deputy Assistant Secretary for Policy
3623	Deputy Assistant Secretary for Planning and Evaluation
3624	Immediate Office of Assistance Secretary for Policy and Planning
3625	Deputy Assistant Secretary for Budget
3627	Deputy Assistant Secretary for Financial Management
3628	Immediate Office of Assistant Secretary for Management
3630	Under Secretary for Memorial Affairs / National Cemetery System
3632	Deputy Assistant Secretary for Diversity and Equal Employment Opportunity
3633	Director – Office of Administration
3634	Deputy Assistant Secretary for Human Resources Management and Labor Relations
3636	Immed. Office – Assist. Sec'y for Public & Intergov. Affairs
3637	Deputy Assistant Secretary for Intergovernmental Affairs and International Affairs
3638	Deputy Assistant Secretary for Public Affairs
3640	Under Secretary for Benefits / Veterans Benefit Administration
3641	Deputy Assist. Sec'y for Office of Resolution Management
3643	Deputy Assist. Sec'y for Acquisition and Materiel Management
3646	Immediate Office of Assistant Secretary for Congressional and and Legislative Affairs
3644	Director – Asset Enterprise Management
3645	Associate Deputy for Labor - Management Relations
3647	Director, Congressional Affairs
3648	Deputy Assistant Secretary for Legislative Affairs
3649	Immed. Office – Assist. Sec'y - Human Resources & Admin.
3650	Assistant Secretary for Information and Technology
3651	Immediate Office of the Assist. Sec. – Info. & Technology
3652	Deputy Assistant Sec. For Information & Technology
3655	Deputy Assistant Secretary for Security Preparedness
3656	Deputy Assistant Secretary for Security and Law Enforcement
4100	Merit Systems Protection Board
4500	Equal Employment Opportunity Commission
4567	Interagency Committee on Employment of People with Disabilities
4602	Appalachian Regional Commission
4607	Interstate Commission on the Potomac River Basin
4608	The Port Authority of NY and NJ
4609	Washington Metropolitan Area Transit Authority

TABLE OF ORGANIZATIONS AND CODES

Code Organization

4700	**GENERAL SERVICES ADMINISTRATION**
4701	Immediate Office of the Administrator
4703	Office of General Counsel
4704	Office of Inspector General
4705	Office of the Chief People Officer
4707	Office of Congressional and Intergovernmental Affairs
4708	Office of Citizen Services and Communications
4712	GSA Board of Contract Appeals
4717	Office of the Chief Financial Officer
4722	Offices of the Regional Administrators
4724	Office of Civil Rights
4728	Office of Small Business Utilization
4732	Office of the Federal Acquisition Service
4740	Public Buildings Service
4743	Office of Childcare
4745	Office of Governmentwide Policy
4750	Office of the Chief Information Officer
4760	Office of the Chief Acquisition Officer
4808	National Bipartisan Commission on the Future of Medicare
4817	State Justice Institute
4827	Commission on Ocean Policy
4835	Medicare Payment Advisory Commission
4836	Commission on Executive, Legislative and Judicial Salaries
4849	Office of Navajo and Hopi Indian Relocation
4856	Nuclear Waste Technical Review Board
4860	United State-China Economic and Security Review Commission
4864	U.S. Commission on International Religious Freedom
4900	NATIONAL SCIENCE FOUNDATION
4960	National Science Board
4965	Arctic Research Commission
49SA	International Astronomical Union
49SB	International Union of Biological Sciences
49SC	International Union of Pure and Applied Chemistry
49SD	International Union of Geodesy and Geophysics
49SE	International Geological Union
49SF	International Union of Pure and Applied Physics
49SG	International Geographical Union
49SK	International Union of Biochemistry & Molecular Biology
49SM	International Mathematical Union

TABLE OF ORGANIZATIONS AND CODES

Code Organization

49SN   International Union of Nutritional Sciences
49SO   International Commission on Optics
49SP   International Union of Physiological Sciences
49SQ   International Union for Quaternary Research
49SR   International Union of Radio Sciences
49SS   International Union of Psychological Science
49ST   International Union of Theoretical and Applied Mechanics
49SU International Council of Scientific Unions
49SV   International Union for Pure and Applied Biophysics
49SW International Union of Microbiological Societies
49SX   International Union of Crystallography
49SY   Pacific Science Association
49SZ   Committee on Science and Technology for Development

5000   Securities and Exchange Commission
5094   Securities Investor Protection Corporation

5100   Federal Deposit Insurance Corporation

5400   Federal Labor Relations Authority

5600 Central   Intelligence Agency

5700   **AIR FORCE**, Department of the (Headquarters, USAF)
5701   Air Force Management Engineering Agency
5702   Air Force Inspection and Safety Center
5703   Air Force Operational Test and Evaluation Center
5704   Air Force Communications Agency
5705   Air Force Intelligence Service
5706   Air Force Audit Agency
5707   Air Force Office of Special Investigations
5708   Air Force Office of Security Police
5709   Air Force Personnel Center
5711   Air Force Manpower Agency
570B   U.S. Air Force Academy
570D   U.S. Air Forces, Europe
570I   Air Reserve Personnel Center
570J   Air Training Command
570K   Air University
570M   Headquarters, Air Force Reserve
570N   Immediate Office, Headquarters, USAF

TABLE OF ORGANIZATIONS AND CODES

Code Organization

570R	Pacific Air Forces
570U	Air Force Headquarters Air Intelligence Agency
570Y	Air Force Communications Command
571A	Air Force C2 & Intelligence, Surveillance, & Reconnaissance
571C	Air Combat Command
571G	Air Force Logistics Management Agency
571L	Air Mobility Command
571M	Air Force Materiel Command
571O	Air Force Center for Quality and Management Innovation
571P	Air Force Real Property Agency
571Q	HQ AF Flight Standards Agency
571S	Space Command
571W	Air Force Engineering and Services Center
5727	Air Force Agency for Modeling and Simulation
5728	Air Force Communication and Information Center
5729	Air Force National Security Emergency Preparedness
572A	Air Force Cost Center
572B	Air Force Doctrine Center
572C	Air Force Civilian Personnel Management Center
572D	Air Force Personnel Operations Agency
572E	Air Force Legal Services Center
572F	Air Force Medical Services Center
572G	Air Force Service Information and News Center
572H	Air Force Combat Operations Staff
572I	Air National Guard Support Center
572K	U.S. Air Force Historical Research Center
572L	Air Force Technical Applications Center
572M	Air Force Review Boards Office
572N	Air Force Center for Studies and Analyses
572P	Air Force Center for International Programs
572Q	Air Weather Service
572R	Air Force Program Executive Office
572S	HQ NORAD
572T	Air Force Supply Center
572U	Air Force Morale, Welfare and Recreation Center
572V	Air Force Disposal Agency
572W	Air Force District of Washington
572X	Air Force Real Estate Agency
572Y	Air Force Pentagon Communications. Agency
572Z	HQ Air Force Medical Operations Agency
5734	Air National Guard Units (Mobilization) (Title 5)
573C	Air Force Elements, U.S. Central Command

TABLE OF ORGANIZATIONS AND CODES

Code Organization

573D	Air Force Elements, U.S. Special Operations Command
573G	Air Force Elements, Europe
573I	Reservist, Centrally Managed
573K	HQ U.S. European Command
573L	Center for Air Force History
573M	Air Force Elements, U.S. Southern Command
573N	Air Force Elements, U.S. Atlantic Command
573O	Air Force Elements, U.S. Pacific Command
573Q	Air Force Elements, U.S. Strategic Command
573R	Air Force Elements, U.S. Readiness Command
573S	Headquarters, U.S. Space Command and NORAD
573T	Air Force Elements U.S. Transportation Command
573V	Air Force Elements, Other than Europe
573W	Air Force Center for Environmental Excellence
573Y	Air Force Frequency Management Center
573Z	Joint Services Survival, Evasion, Resistance and Escape Agency
574Z	Air National Guard
57NG	Air National Guard Units (Title 32)
57ZG	U.S. Special Operations Command (ANG Title 32)
57ZS	U.S. Special Operations Command (Air Force)

5900	NATIONAL FOUNDATION ON THE ARTS AND THE HUMANITIES
5915	Federal Council on the Arts and the Humanities
5920	National Endowment for the Arts
5940	National Endowment for the Humanities
5950	Institute of Museum Services
5963	National Council on the Arts
5966	National Council on the Humanities

6000	Railroad Retirement Board
6100	Consumer Product Safety Commission
6201	Office of Special Counsel
6300	National Labor Relations Board
6400	Tennessee Valley Authority
6500	Federal Maritime Commission

TABLE OF ORGANIZATIONS AND CODES

Code Organization

6800	**ENVIRONMENTAL PROTECTION AGENCY**
6801	Immediate Office of the Administrator of EPA
6802	Deputy Administrator
6803	Office of General Counsel
6804	Office of the Inspector General
6805	Assistant Administrator for Administration and Resources Management
6809	Assistant Administrator for International Affairs
680S	Office of the Administrator of EPA
6820	Assistant Administrator for Air and Radiation
6825	Assistant Administrator for Enforcement and Compliance Assurance
6830	Assistant Administrator for Prevention, Pesticides, and Toxic Substances
6840	Assistant Administrator for Research and Development
6845	Assistant Administrator for Water
6850	Assistant Administrator for Solid Waste and Emergency Response
6853	Office of the Chief Financial Officer
6860	Commission on Risk Assessment and Risk Management
68SA	Associate Administrator for Office of Public Affairs
68SB	Associate Administrator for Congressional and Intergovernmental Relations
68SC	Office of Homeland Security
68SD	Environmental Appeals Board
68SE	Executive Secretariat
68SF	Office of Executive Services
68SG	Office of Administrative Law Judges
68SH	Office of Civil Rights
68SJ	Office of Cooperative Environmental Management
68SK	Office of Small and Disadvantaged Business Utilization
68SL	Office of Policy, Economics and Innovation
68SM	Science Advisory Board
6900	**TRANSPORTATION**, Department of
6901	Immediate Office of the Secretary of Transportation
6902	Associate Deputy Secretary/ Office of Intermodalism
6903	Office of General Counsel
6904	Office of Inspector General
6905	Assistant Secretary for Administration
6906	Assist. Secretary for Budget and Programs/Chief Financial Officer
6907	Assistant Secretary for Governmental Affairs
6908	Assistant Secretary - Office of Public Affairs
6909	Assistant Secretary for Transportation Policy

TABLE OF ORGANIZATIONS AND CODES

Code Organization

6910   Office of the Chief Information Officer

690S   Office of the Secretary of Transportation
6911   Office of Civil Rights
6912   Board of Contract Appeals
6913   Office of Commercial Space Transportation
6914   Executive Secretariat
6915   Office of Intelligence, Security and Emergency Response
6917   Deputy Secretary of Transportation
6916   Office of Drug and Alcohol Policy and Compliance
6918   OSDBU/Minority Business Resources Center
6920   Federal Aviation Administration
6922   Assistant Secretary for Aviation and International Affairs
6925   Federal Highway Administration
6930   Federal Railroad Administration
6938 Maritime   Administration
6940   National Highway Traffic Safety Administration
6943   Research and Innovative Technology Administration
6947   Saint Lawrence Seaway Development Corporation
6953   Federal Motor Carrier Safety Administration
6955   Federal Transit Administration
6957   Pipeline and Hazardous Materials Safety Administration
6959   Surface Transportation Board - formerly ICC – code 3000
6991   National Railroad Passenger Corporation (AMTRAK)

7000 HOMELAND   SECURITY, Department of

7001   Office of the Secretary, Department of Homeland Security
7002   Immediate Office of the Secretary
7003   U.S. Citizenship and Immigration Services
7004   Office of the Inspector General
7008   U.S. Coast Guard
7009   U.S. Secret Service
7012   U.S. Immigration and Customs Enforcement
7013   Transportation Security Administration
7014   U.S. Customs and Border Protection
7015   Federal Law Enforcement Training Center
7022   Federal Emergency Management Agency
7032   Office for Information Analysis
7033   Office for Infrastructure Protection
7040   Under Secretary for Science and Technology

TABLE OF ORGANIZATIONS AND CODES

Code Organization

7041   Office of the Under Secretary for Science and Technology
7050   Under Secretary for Management
7051   Office of the Under Secretary for Management

7100   Overseas Private Investment Corporation

7200   U.S. Agency for International Development

7300   Small Business Administration
7360   National Women's Business Council

7400   American Battle Monuments Commission

7500   **HEALTH AND HUMAN SERVICES**, Department of

7501   Immediate Office of the Secretary of Health and Human Services
7502   Office of the Deputy Secretary of Health and Human Services
7503   Office of the General Counsel
7504   Office of the Inspector General
7505   Office of Assistant Secretary for Administration and Management
7506   Office of Assistant Secretary for Planning and Evaluation
7507   Office of Assistant Secretary for Legislation
7508   Office of Assistant Secretary for Public Affairs
7509   Office of Intergovernmental Affairs and Regional Directors
7510   Office of the Assistant Secretary for Resources and Technology
750S   Office of the Secretary of Health and Human Services
7511   Office for Civil Rights
7512   Office of Assistant Secretary for Public Response
7515   Office of Public Health and Science
7516   Departmental Appeals Board
7520   Public Health Service
7521   Office of the Surgeon General
7522   Substance Abuse and Mental Health Services Administration
7523   Centers for Disease Control and Prevention
7524   Food and Drug Administration
7525   Agency for Toxic Substances and Disease Registry
7526   Health Resources and Services Administration
7527   Indian Health Service
7528   Agency for Healthcare Research and Quality
7529   National Institutes of Health
7530 Centers   for Medicare & Medicaid Services
7545   Administration on Aging

TABLE OF ORGANIZATIONS AND CODES

Code Organization

7555   Program Support Center
7590   Administration for Children and Families
7635   Christopher Columbus Fellowship Foundation

7800 Farm   Credit Administration
7881   Bank for Cooperatives
7884   Farm Credit Banks
7886   Farm Credit System Financial Assistance Corporation
7888   Farm Credit System Insurance Corporation
7889   Federal Agricultural Mortgage Corporation (Farmer Mac)

8000   **NATIONAL AERONAUTICS AND SPACE ADMINISTRATION**
8001 Headquarters,   NASA
8020   Ames Research Center
8022   Dryden Flight Research Center
8025   NASA Shared Services Center
8026   Goddard Space Flight Center
8029   NASA Management Office, Jet Propulsion Laboratory
8032   Lyndon B. Johnson Space Center
8035   John F. Kennedy Space Center
8038   Langley Research Center
8041   John H. Glenn Research Center at Lewis Field
8044   George C. Marshall Space Flight Center
8047   John C. Stennis Space Center

8291   Neighborhood Reinvestment Corporation

8300   Export-Import Bank of the U.S.

8400   United States Soldiers' and Airmen's Home
84AF   Armed Forces Retirement Home

8600   **HOUSING AND URBAN DEVELOPMENT**, Department of
8601   Office of the Secretary of Housing and Urban Development
8602   Deputy Secretary of Housing and Urban Development
8603   Office of General Counsel
8604   Office of Inspector General
8605 Assistant   Secretary for Administration
8606   Office of Chief Financial Officer
8607   Assistant Secretary for Congressional and Intergovernmental Relations
8608   Assistant Secretary for Public Affairs

TABLE OF ORGANIZATIONS AND CODES

Code Organization

8611   Assistant Secretary for Fair Housing and Equal Opportunity
8613   HUD Board of Contract Appeals
8615   Office of Administrative Law Judges
8617   Office of Small and Disadvantaged Business Utilization
8620   Assistant Secretary for Community Planning and Development
8622   Assistant Deputy Secretary for Field Policy and Management
8625 Government   National Mortgage Association (Ginnie Mae)
8627   Office of Departmental Equal Employment Opportunity
8630 Assistant   Secretary for Housing--Federal Housing Commissioner
8635   Assistant Secretary for Public and Indian Housing
8645   Assistant Secretary for Policy Development and Research
8651   Office of Departmental Operations and Coordination
8652   Office of the Chief Information Officer
8653   Office Healthy Homes and Lead Hazard Control
8654   Office of the Chief Procurement Officer
8656   Office of Federal Housing Enterprise Oversight
8658   Center for Faith-based and Community Initiatives
8659   Office of Field Policy and Management
865A   Office of the Field Policy and Management Region I, Boston Regional Office
865B   Office of the Field Policy and Management Region II, New York Regional Office
865C   Office of the Field Policy and Management Region III, Philadelphia Regional
              Office
865D   Office of Field Policy and Management Region IV, Atlanta Regional Office
865E   Office of Field Policy and Management Region V, Chicago Regional Office
865F   Office of Field Policy and Management Region VI, Fort Worth Regional Office
865G   Office of Field Policy and Management Region VII, Kansas City Regional Office
865H   Office of Field Policy and Management Region VIII, Denver Regional Office
865J   Office of Field Policy and Management Region IX, San Francisco Regional Office
865K   Office of Field Policy and Management Region X, Seattle Regional Office

8681   Federal National Mortgage Association (Fannie Mae)
8683   Federal Home Loan Mortgage Corporation (Freddie Mac)

8800   NATIONAL ARCHIVES AND RECORDS ADMINISTRATION
8852   Information Security Oversight Office
8861   National Archives Trust Fund Board
8862   National Historical Publications and Records Commission
8865   Administrative Committee of the Federal Register

TABLE OF ORGANIZATIONS AND CODES

Code Organization

8900	**ENERGY**, Department of
8901	Office of the Secretary
8903	Office of the General Counsel
8904	Office of the Inspector General
8905	Assistant Secretary for Congressional and Intergovernmental Affairs
8906	Office of Hearings and Appeals
8911	Office of Civilian Radioactive Waste Management
8915	Office of Public Affairs
8917	Assistant Secretary for Environmental Management
8921	Assistant Secretary for Energy Efficiency and Renewable Energy
8925	Office of Science
8927	Office of Nuclear Energy, Science and Technology
8928	Assistant Secretary for Fossil Energy
8929	Office of Intelligence
8932	Office the of the Energy Information Administration
8936	Office of Legacy Management
8938	Assistant Secretary for Policy and International Affairs
8955	Consolidated Business Center
8974	Strategic Petroleum Reserves
8981	Casper Naval Pet & Oil Shale Reserves
8982	Elk Hills Naval Pet & Oil Shale Reserves
8990	Federal Energy Regulatory Commission
891C	Office of Economic Impact and Diversity
891H	Office of Health, Safety and Security
891N	Office of the Chief Information Officer
891S	Office of the Departmental Representative to the Defense Nuclear Facilities Safety Board
892E	Office of the Secretary of Energy Advisory Board Support Office
892H	Office of Counterintelligence
892L	Office of Electricity Delivery and Energy Reliability
893C	Office of the Chief Financial Officer
893H	Office of Human Capital Management
893M	Office of Management
89AL	Albuquerque Operations Office (non-NNSA) (EM)
89BA	Chicago Office
89BB	Oak Ridge Office
89BC	Ames Site Office
89BD	Argonne Site Office
89BE	Berkeley Site Office
89BF	Brookhaven Site Office
89BG	Fermi Site Office
89BH	Pacific Northwest Site Office

TABLE OF ORGANIZATIONS AND CODES

Code Organization

89BI	Princeton Site Office
89BJ	Stanford Site Office
89BK	Thomas Jefferson Site Office
89BP	Bonneville Power Marketing Administration
89CB	Carlsbad Field Office
89GO	Golden Field Office
89ID	Idaho Operations Office
89N0	Deputy Under Secretary for Counterterrorism
89N1	Deputy Administration for Defense Programs
89N2	Deputy Administrator for Defense Nuclear Nonproliferation
89N3	Deputy Administrator for Naval Reactors
89N4	Office of Emergency Operations
89N5	Associate Administrator for Facilities and Operations
89N6	Associate Administrator for Management and Administration
89N7	Associate Administrator for Defense Nuclear Security
89NA	Office of Nuclear Security/National Nuclear Security Administration
89NE	National Energy Technology Laboratory
89NV	Nevada Operations Office (non-National Nuclear Security Administration) (Environmental Management)
89NW	Oakland Operations Office (non-National Nuclear Security Administration) (Environmental Management)
89OH	Ohio Field Office
89PP	Portsmouth and Paducah Project Office
89RF	Rocky Flats Project Office
89RL	Richland Operations Office
89RP	Office of River Protection
89SE	Southeastern Power Marketing Administration
89SR	Savannah River Operations Office
89SV	Savannah River Site Office
89SW	Southwestern Power Marketing Administration
89WA	Western Area Power Marketing Administration
89X1	Pittsburgh Naval Reactors
89X2	Schenectady Naval Reactors
89XQ	Y-12 Site Office
89XR	Pantex Site Office
89XS	Sandia Site Office
89XT	Kansas City Site Office
89XU	Los Alamos Site Office
89XV	Nevada Site Office
89XW	Livermore Site Office
89ZA	National Nuclear Security Administration Service Center

TABLE OF ORGANIZATIONS AND CODES

Code Organization

9000   Selective Service System

9100   **EDUCATION**, Department of
9101   Immediate Office of the Secretary of Education
9102   Office of the Deputy Secretary of Education
9103   Office of the General Counsel
9104   Office of Inspector General
9105   Office of Management
9106   Office of the Chief Financial Officer
9107   Office of Legislation and Congressional Affairs
9108   Office of the Under Secretary
9109   Office of Office of Communications and Outreach
9110   Office of Planning, Evaluation and Program Development
9111   Office for Civil Rights
9115   Office of the Chief Information Officer
9120   Office of Vocational and Adult Education
9121   Office of English Language Acquisition
9124   Office of Special Education and Rehabilitative Services
9125   National Institute on Disability and Rehabilitation Research
9126   Rehabilitation Services Administration
9127   Office of Special Education Programs
9128   Immed. Office – Assist. Sec'y for Spec. Ed. & Rehab. Services
9129   Fund for the Improvement of Postsecondary Education
9130   Immediate Office of the Assist. Sec'y for Postsecondary Education
9131   Federal Student Aid
9132   Immediate Office of the Director of Education Sciences
9133   Office of Higher Education Programs
9134   Office of Postsecondary Education
9135   National Center for Education Research
9136   National Center for Special Education Research
9137   National Center for Educational Evaluation and Regional Assistance
9138   National Center for Education Statistics
9139   Institute of Education Sciences
9140   Student Achievement and School Accountability Program
9141   Immed. Office – Assist. Sec'y for Elementary & Secondary Ed.
9142   Migrant Education Programs
9143   School Support and Technology Programs
9144   Impact Aid Programs
9145   Office of Indian Education
9146   Office of Elementary and Secondary Education
9147   Academic Improvement and Teacher Quality Programs

96

TABLE OF ORGANIZATIONS AND CODES

Code Organization

9150   Office of Innovation and Improvement
9155   Office of Safe and Drug-Free Schools
916A   Advisory Councils and Committees
916B   National Assessment Governing Board
916C   National Institute for Literacy
916D   Federal Interagency Committee on Education
9181   Student Loan Marketing Association (Sallie Mae)
9182   College Construction Loan Insurance Association (Connie Lee)
9191   American Printing House for the Blind
9192 Gallaudet   University
9193 Howard   University
9194   National Technical Institute for the Deaf

9300   Federal Mediation and Conciliation Service

9502   National Capital Planning Commission
9504   Federal Mine Safety and Health Review Commission
9506   Federal Election Commission
9507   Commodity Futures Trading Commission
9508   National Transportation Safety Board
9509   National Council on Disability
9510   Harry S. Truman Scholarship Foundation
9512 Japan-U.S.   Friendship Commission
9513 Marine Mammal   Commission
9514   Occupational Safety and Health Review Commission
9516   Defense Nuclear Facilities Safety Board
9517   Commission on Civil Rights
9518   Committee for Purchase from People who are Blind or Severely Disabled
9522   Centennial of Flight Commission
9523   Election Assistance Commission
9524 National Mediation   Board
9525   National Counterintelligence Center
9527   National Commission on Libraries and Information Science
9528   Office of the Federal Coordinator Alaska Natural Gas Transportation Projects
9530   Advisory Council On Historic Preservation
9531   United States Holocaust Memorial Museum
9532   Architectural and Transportation Barriers Compliance Board
9535   Institute of Am. Indian and Alaska Native Culture and Arts Development
9537   Commission of Fine Arts
9540   Federal Housing Finance Board
9541   James Madison Memorial Fellowship Foundation
9543   Millennium Challenge Corporation

TABLE OF ORGANIZATIONS AND CODES

Code Organization

9545   Morris K. Udall Scholar. & Excellence in Nat'l Enviro. Policy Foundation
9547   Delta Regional Authority
9549   Office of Government Ethics
9554   Interagency Council on the Homeless
9555   National Communications System
9559   Federal Reserve System, Board of Governors
9560   Barry Goldwater Scholarship and Excellence in Education Foundation
9562 Federal   Financial Institutions Examination Council
9565   Chemical Safety and Hazard Investigation Board
9567   Commission for the Preservation of America's Heritage Abroad
9568   Broadcasting Board of Governors
9570 Presidio   Trust
9572 Delani   Commission
9574   White House Commission on the National Moment of Remembrance
9577 Corporation   for National and Community Service
9580   United States Institute of Peace
9585   Financing Corporation (FICO)
9589   United Mine Workers of America Benefit Funds
9590   Valles Caldera Trust
9591   Vietnam Education Foundation
9593   U.S. Court of Veterans Appeals
9594   Court Services and Offender Supervision Agency for the District of Columbia
959D   Office of the Director – CSOSA
959P   Pretrial Services Agency - CSOSA

95HL   Federal Home Loan Banks
9668   Mississippi River Commission
96CE   U.S. Army Corps of Engineers - civil program financing only
96NC Permanent   International Association of Navigation Congresses
96RC Permanent   International Association of Road Congresses

9700   **DEFENSE**, Department of (except military departments)
9736   Army/Air Force Exchange Service
9748   Defense Human Resources Activity
9758   Defense Prisoner of War/Missing Personnel Office
9759   Consolidated Metropolitan Technical Personnel Center
9760   TRICARE Management Activity
9761   Defense Threat Reduction Agency
9762   Defense Career Management and Support Agency
9763   Defense Contract Management Agency

TABLE OF ORGANIZATIONS AND CODES

Code Organization

9765	Pentagon Force Protection Agency
9766	Department of Defense Counterintelligence Field Activity
9767	Unified Combatant Command Headquarters
9769	National Defense University
9770	Armed Forces Radiobiology Research Institute
9771	Defense Microelectronics Activity
9772	Pentagon Renovation Program Office
9773	Virginia Contracting Activity
9774	Defense Technical Information Center
97AB	National Geospatial-Intelligence Agency
97AD	Office of the Secretary of Defense
97AE	Defense Advanced Research Projects Agency
97AK	Defense Information Systems Agency
97AQ	Defense Legal Services Agency
97AR	Defense Contract Audit Agency
97AS	Defense Logistics Agency
97AT	Defense Security Cooperation Agency
97AU	Defense Technology Security Administration
97AV	Defense Security Service
97AZ	Defense Commissary Agency
97BJ	Organization of the Joint Chiefs of Staff
97BZ	Defense Finance and Accounting Service
97CG	National Security Agency/Central Security Service
97DL	Defense Intelligence Agency
97EX	Office of the Inspector General
97F1	American Forces Information Service
97F2	Department of Defense Education Activity
97F5	Washington Headquarters Services
97F6	Office of Economic Adjustment
97GZ	U.S. Court of Appeals for the Armed Forces
97JC	Missile Defense Agency
97NH	United States Naval Home

Appendix A   Incorporated Changes

The following codes have been incorporated in this publication:

9528   Office of the Federal Coordinator Alaska Natural Gas Transportation Projects (new)
7521   Office of the Surgeon General (Name change)
7505   Office of Assistant Secretary for Administration and Management (Name change)
7510   Office of Assistant Secretary for Resources and Technology (new)
7512   Office of Assistant Secretary for Public Response (new)
8906   Office of Hearings and Appeals (Name change)

www.ingramcontent.com/pod-product-compliance
Lightning Source LLC
LaVergne TN
LVHW060123070326
832902LV00019B/3112